CAREER SKILLS LIBRARY

Communication Skills

THIRD EDITION

CAREER SKILLS LIBRARY

Communication Skills

Finding A Job

Leadership Skills

Learning the Ropes

Organization Skills

Problem Solving

Professional Ethics and Etiquette

Research and Information Management

Teamwork Skills

FERGUSON

CAREER SKILLS LIBRARY

Communication Skills

THIRD EDITION

Ferguson Publishing
An imprint of Infobase Publishing

Communication Skills, Third Edition

Copyright © 1998, 2004, 2009 by Infobase Publishing

Ferguson
An imprint of Infobase Publishing
132 West 31st Street
New York NY 10001

Library of Congress Cataloging-in-Publication Data

Communication skills. — 3rd ed.
    p. cm. — (Career skills library)
    Includes bibliographical references and index.
    ISBN-13: 978-0-8160-7778-6 (hardcover : alk. paper)
    ISBN-10: 0-8160-7778-9 (hardcover : alk. paper) 1. Business communication. 2. Commercial correspondence. 3. Public speaking. 4. Listening. I. Worth, Richard. Communication skills.
    HF5718.W67 2009
    651.7—dc22
                                    2009006664

Ferguson books are available at special discounts when purchased in bulk quantities for businesses, associations, institutions, or sales promotions. Please call our Special Sales Department in New York at (212) 967-8800 or (800) 322-8755.

You can find Ferguson on the World Wide Web at http://www.fergpubco.com

Text design by David Strelecky, adapted by Erik Lindstrom
Cover design by Takeshi Takahashi
First edition by Joe Mackall

Printed in the United States of America

MP ML 10 9 8 7 6 5 4 3 2 1

This book is printed on acid-free paper.

CONTENTS

INTRODUCTION

Communication is a vital part of our daily routines. We sit in school and listen to teachers. We read books and magazines. We talk to friends, watch television, and communicate over the Internet.

The workplace is no different. Experts tell us that 70–80 percent of our working time is spent in some kind of communication. We're reading and writing memos, sending and responding to emails, listening to our coworkers, or having one-to-one conversations with our supervisors.

Communication involves at least two people: the sender and the receiver. In this book, we'll look at four types of communication between senders and receivers: writing, speaking, listening, and conducting meetings. Each one is important to your success in the workplace.

For example, a poorly written cover letter can prevent you from being hired for a job. On the other hand, the ability to write effectively and make clear presentations can make the difference between your being promoted or being left behind. As Ken Matejka

DID YOU KNOW?

Employers surveyed in 2007 by the National Association of Colleges and Employers rated communication skills (verbal and written) as very-to-extremely important for job candidates.

and Diane Ramos explain in their book *Hook 'Em: Speaking and Writing to Catch and Keep a Business Audience,* "You need effective, persuasive communication skills for career advancement."

A communication skill that's often overlooked is listening. Yet recent surveys tell us that we spend 45 percent of our time listening. Do we listen carefully to what people are telling us? According to one study, we hear only one quarter of what's being said. The rest of the time we're daydreaming or just tuned out completely.

One sales manager in a printing company tells the story of needing a job rushed through in 24 hours so his best customer could have it on time. He gave careful instructions about the project to the production supervisor. But before he could finish, the supervisor had already stopped listening. He assumed that the customer wanted the job three days later, which was the usual deadline for most of these projects. When the sales manager went to pick up the job the next day, it wasn't ready. As a result, he almost lost the customer. Unfortunately, stories like these are common in many organizations.

HOW WE SPEND OUR COMMUNICATION TIME

Writing	9%
Reading	16%
Talking	30%
Listening	45%

Listening, writing, and speaking are all skills we use in meetings.

Listening, writing, and speaking are all skills we use in meetings. Today, meetings are a common method for making decisions. More and more work is done by teams of people who come from different areas of a company. They accomplish many of their tasks in team meetings. In these situations, we must be able to speak and write clearly so others can understand us and listen carefully to what they say. Sadly, we waste many hours in meetings because of poor communication. A study by one university estimated that $37 billion is lost annually through unproductive meetings.

Strong communication skills are vital in the field of photo-styling. This profession involves the envisioning and creative assimilation of many ideas from different people and sources. Concepts can be very vague and subjective, hence there is a large margin for error and misinterpretation. The process works best when discussions are clear and there is plenty of information.

—**Carey Cornelius, photo stylist**

Whether you're writing, listening, speaking, or attending meetings, communication skills are critical to your success in the workplace. In this book, we'll look at some of the skills that will enable your communications to be more successful. These include:

- Understanding the purpose of a communication
- Analyzing the audience
- Communicating with words as well as with body language
- Giving each communication greater impact

WRITING WITH A PURPOSE

Jill's boss asked her to write a memo on a school-to-work program. The company where Jill worked was a leader in the computer software field. A school-to-work program would give young people in school a chance to be employed part time and to learn the software business. If their work was good, the company might hire them for full-time jobs after they graduated.

"Keep the memo short," Jill's boss told her. "And stick to the point."

Jill was supposed to explain the type of program her company should start. She sat down at her computer and began to write. On the first page, she talked about her own experience in a school-to-work program. Then she described what two of her friends had done in their programs. They had worked part time in other companies. Next she wrote about several school-to-work programs described in magazines. Five pages later, she finally signed her name.

✔ TRUE OR FALSE?

Do You Know How to Write with a Purpose?

1. When writing for others, it's important to know your reader.

2. There are three keys, known as the 3 Cs, to a successful resume: concise, clear, and correct.

3. Cover letters can be up to two pages in length.

4. It's okay for business emails to have typos and be full of slang.

Test yourself as you read through this chapter. The answers appear on pages 47, 48, and 50.

"Well, I think the information my boss wants is in here somewhere," she said to herself. Then she submitted the memo.

To write well, express yourself like common people, but think like a wise man. Or, think as wise men do, but speak as common people do.

—Aristotle, Greek philosopher

Jill's boss was a busy person. He received more than 50 memos each day, and he didn't have time to read every memo completely. A memo writer had to get to the point quickly. Otherwise, Jill's boss would read no further. He read the first paragraph of Jill's memo. Then he scanned the second paragraph.

"What's the point of this memo?" he asked himself. He threw up his hands in frustration and threw the memo away.

INFORMATION OVERLOAD

In the workplace, information seems to come from all directions. Each day, managers are expected to read memos, letters, and reports. Correspondence

It is important to have a clear purpose when writing any type of document. (Helen King/ Torrance, CA USA, Corbis)

arrives through email, fax, and overnight delivery. With so much information coming in, managers don't have time to read all of it. Often they will stop reading a memo if it doesn't capture their interest quickly.

DID YOU KNOW?

Eighty-one percent of employers surveyed by The Conference Board in 2006 rated high school graduates as deficient in written communication skills.

Source: *Are They Really Ready to Work?*

How can you make sure that people will read your memo? How can you be certain that your boss will remember what you have written? You must have a clear purpose and state that purpose as quickly as possible. This was something that Jill neglected to do in her memo. It's also essential that you know your readers and give them the information they want. Jill's boss wanted a concise memo that explained the type of school-to-work program the company should adopt. Instead, Jill gave him a rambling five-page report that didn't tell him what he wanted to know. As a result, it ended up in the wastebasket.

You must have a clear purpose and state that purpose as quickly as possible.

☞ FACT

The average worker receives approximately 75 email, phone, and mail contacts each day.

DEFINE YOUR PURPOSE

Many people just sit down, begin writing, and hope for the best. Sometimes they are lucky. However, most of the time they produce poorly written and confusing material. Before you begin writing, state your purpose and how you propose to carry it out. This information can be stated briefly in one or two summary sentences. These sentences sum up the purpose of your writing.

If you cannot express in a sentence or two what you intend to get across, then it is not focused well enough.

—Charles Osgood, TV commentator

Suppose you want your school to sponsor a class trip. You decide to write a letter to the principal about it. Here are your summary sentences:

My letter is designed to persuade the principal to sponsor the trip. The letter will present three reasons why the trip would be valuable for students.

The purpose of some writing is to *persuade*. We use this type of writing both at school and on the job. Jan believed that her office needed more computers. Without them, she and her coworkers simply couldn't keep up with the volume of their work. Jan wrote a memo to her boss to persuade him to purchase additional computers. She pointed out that everyone would get more work done if there were more computers to use. She also found a company that sold computers at a low price. Jan's arguments and initial research convinced her boss to buy the computers.

The purpose of other writing is to *explain.* Holly worked part time at a pet store that sold fish. She had to write a memo for new employees on how to feed each type of fish. Here are her summary sentences:

DOS AND DON'TS OF SUMMARY SENTENCES

Do

- Write summary sentences before doing anything else.
- Keep your sentences short.
- Specify whether the purpose of your writing is to persuade, explain, or describe.

Don't

- Exceed one or two sentences for each writing project.
- Include any information in your paper that doesn't relate to the summary sentences.

✍️ EXERCISE

Write one or two summary sentences for a short paper that accomplish the following:

- explains how to be a successful student.
- persuades an employer to hire you for a part-time job.
- describes what happened at an important meeting you attended as part of an extracurricular activity.
- details a trip you took during your summer vacation.
- describes a movie you recently watched.

My memo explains the feeding times for each fish. It also explains the type of food and quantity of food that each fish should receive.

Some writing is primarily designed to *describe*. Robert's supervisor sent him to a conference and wanted him to write a memo describing what happened there. Robert knew his supervisor didn't want to know everything that occurred but only the most important things. Here is Robert's summary sentence:

I will describe the three significant things I learned at the conference that might help our department.

☞ FACT

An estimated 85 percent of our success in business is determined by our communication skills.

WRITING FOR YOUR READER

Some people keep diaries or journals. This type of writing is meant only for themselves. However, most writing is meant for others to read. Thus, it's important for you, as the writer, to know as much as

QUESTIONS TO ASK ABOUT YOUR READERS

Who are they?

What do they need to know about the topic?

What is their attitude toward the topic?

Why should they care about the topic?

possible about your readers. Knowing your readers will help you decide what to say and how to say it.

A human resources manager at a manufacturing company explains that some new employees often don't understand the "politics" of the organization. Suppose they think a supervisor is treating them unfairly. They're apt to fire off a memo telling him about it. Unfortunately, these employees don't last very long in the organization. You may be able to complain to your coworkers about unfair treatment, but new employees are not expected to criticize their boss.

Before you send off a memo or a letter, it is very important to understand your readers.

Before you send off a memo or a letter, it is very important to understand your readers. Ask yourself what you can say, what you can't say, and what your reader expects of you.

Some supervisors are interested in facts and figures only. Suppose you are proposing a new project. Your supervisor may only want to know how it will benefit the organization, how much it will cost, and how you will carry it out. If this is what your supervisor expects, this is what you should give him.

Other supervisors are also interested in learning about the steps you followed in conceptualizing the project. They want to know where you gathered your information and what other companies have undertaken similar projects. They may also be interested in finding out about alternative approaches to executing the project that you considered but later rejected. These supervisors are more process oriented and detail oriented. If this is the type of supervisor

DOS AND DON'TS OF WRITING FOR YOUR READER

Do

- Remember that all communication is written for your reader.

- Analyze your readers before you begin writing.

- Make your writing appeal to what the reader cares most about.

Don't

- Leave out any important information the reader needs to know.

- Forget that the reader's attitudes will influence how they respond to your writing.

you work for, be sure to give her the information she wants. Otherwise, your project proposal may not be approved.

Another important question to ask yourself when you write is: What information does the reader need to know? Suppose you are writing a letter to apply for a job. You begin the letter this way:

I am applying for the position posted by your department.

Unfortunately, the firm has advertised more than one position in the department. If you don't indicate which position you want, the reader will not be

READ MORE ABOUT IT: WRITING AND WORDS

Bly, Robert W., and Regina Anne Kelly. *The Encyclopedia of Business Letters, Faxes, and Emails: Features Hundreds of Model Letters, Faxes, and Emails to Give Your Business Writing the Attention It Deserves.* Rev. ed. Franklin Lakes, N.J.: Career Press, 2009.

Clark, Roy Peter. *Writing Tools: 50 Essential Strategies for Every Writer.* New York: Little, Brown and Company, 2008.

Editors of The American Heritage Dictionaries. *100 Words Almost Everyone Confuses and Misuses.* Boston: Houghton Mifflin, 2004.

————. *100 Words Every High School Graduate Should Know.* Boston: Houghton Mifflin, 2003.

Fogarty, Mignon. *Grammar Girl's Quick and Dirty Tips for Better Writing.* New York: Holt Paperbacks, 2008.

Griffin, Jack. *How to Say It at Work: Power Words, Phrases, and Communication Secrets for Getting Ahead.* 2d ed. Upper Saddle River, N.J.: Prentice Hall Press, 2008.

Oliu, Walter E., Charles T. Brusaw, and Gerald J. Alred. *Writing That Works: Communicating Effectively on the Job.* 9th ed. Boston: Bedford/St. Martin's, 2006.

Rozakis, Laurie E. *The Complete Idiot's Guide to Grammar and Style.* 2d ed. New York: Alpha, 2003.

able to tell whether you have the proper qualifications. Therefore, you probably will not get the job.

Never assume. One of the biggest mistakes writers make is to assume that their readers have knowledge that they do not have. Suppose you are explaining a complicated procedure on a computer. Do not assume that the reader already understands some of the steps. Be sure to describe everything carefully.

If you are trying to persuade readers to do something, it helps to understand their attitudes. Are they likely to support you? Are they likely to oppose you? Are they neutral? This information helps you decide how persuasive you must be.

PROPOSAL TO THE PRINCIPAL

A group of students wanted to persuade their principal to support a new project. They wanted to have time off for a half day of community service each week. The principal was in favor of community service, but she was opposed to letting students take time away from class to do these projects.

The students explained that the community projects would support what they were learning in school. They realized that the principal was worried that they might lose learning time. Armed with solid knowledge about their reader, they designed arguments that would persuade her. For example, the students explained that by writing reports about the projects, they would improve their communication skills. Some of the projects required them to analyze

✍ EXERCISE

- Write a notice for a club to persuade other students to join it. Keep in mind who your audience is and what their attitudes are.

- Your town is hosting a health education fair, and you have been asked to create a poster advertising it. The challenge is that both teens and senior citizens will be attending. Write descriptive copy for two separate posters—one for teens and one for senior citizens.

- Write about a sporting event at your school. First, write a 500-word summary of the game. Then condense the story down to 250 words, and then 100 words to learn how to write concisely while still conveying all the important details of an event.

and summarize data, and this work would improve their math skills. Given the strength and logic of the students' presentation, the principal agreed to try out one community-service project to see how it worked.

When you write, be sure to ask yourself: What do my readers care about? By mentioning something they care about, you can hook their attention. You can also persuade them to do what you want. Earlier we mentioned a supervisor who cared only about facts and figures. If you write about what she cares about, you may be able to persuade her to adopt your project. Suppose you want to convince other students to join your club. You decide to put a notice up on the bulletin board about an upcoming club meeting. How would you begin the notice in order to hook the readers' attention? The best method is to mention something that they might care about. Perhaps joining the club will enable them to have fun with friends or learn a new skill or make money. Each of these might persuade them to join your club.

THE 4 CS OF SUCCESSFUL WRITING

All good writing starts by defining your purpose and knowing your reader. But that's only the beginning. There are four other elements that you should keep in mind. They are known as the 4 Cs:

1. Concise
2. Compelling
3. Clear
4. Correct

BE CONCISE—THE COVER LETTER

Cover letters (also called job application letters) usually accompany resumes (or résumés, resumés). Both the cover letter and resume are sent to an employer

SURF THE WEB: COVER LETTERS

About.com: Job Searching: Resumes, Cover Letters, and Employment-Related Letters
http://jobsearch.about.com/od/resumes/u/resumesandletters.htm

Career Lab: Cover Letters
http://www.careerlab.com/letters

CareerOneStop: Resumes and Interviews
http://www.jobbankinfo.org

CollegeGrad.com: Cover Letters
http://www.collegegrad.com/coverletters

JobStar Central: About Cover Letters
http://www.jobstar.org/tools/resume/cletters.php

JobWeb: Resumes & Interviews
http://www.jobweb.com/resumes_interviews.aspx

Monster Career Advice: Resume & Letters
http://career-advice.monster.com/resume-tips/home.aspx

Quintessential Careers: Cover Letter Resources for Job-Seekers
http://www.quintcareers.com/covres.html

The Riley Guide: Resumes & Cover Letters
http://www.rileyguide.com/letters.html

Vault.com: Sample Cover Letters
http://www.vault.com/nr/ht_list.jsp?ht_type=9

when you are applying for a job. The resume lists your qualifications for a job in detail, and the cover letter discusses them briefly.

"I had one student," explains career counselor Rozeanne Burt, "who was having a difficult time writing a cover letter. I told him to keep the letter to one page or less and only highlight his most important accomplishments. But he couldn't or wouldn't be selective. Instead he wanted to include everything. He ended up with a letter that ran over a page and a half in tiny, nine-point type. Needless to say, the employer was not impressed and he didn't get the job."

With all the information that employers have to read today, the last thing they want is something long-winded. It's essential to be concise. Human resources director Debby Berggren receives a lot of cover letters from people looking for jobs, and she says that many people have trouble "getting to the point."

If you want to write a concise cover letter, or any other type of letter, it's important to understand the purpose of the letter before you begin writing. In his book *Persuasive Business Proposals: Writing to Win Customers, Clients, and Contracts,* Tom Sant explains that "you will do a better job of writing if you know what you're trying to accomplish: the *why* of a document." By writing one or two summary sentences before you begin writing, you can state the "why" very simply.

DID YOU KNOW?

Cover letters are still an important part of the job search process. Eighty-six percent of executives surveyed by OfficeTeam believe that cover letters are valuable when evaluating job applicants.

If you were to compose your summary sentences for a cover letter, they might sound like this:

My letter persuades an employer to interview me. It includes several of my outstanding accomplishments to convince an employer that I am right for the job.

The purpose of a cover letter is to persuade—to persuade an employer to interview you for a job. The next step is to know your reader. What will the reader find most persuasive? You should list only the experience and skills that you possess that are mostly likely to convince the reader to interview you. As Burt explains: "You can't tell them everything about you, so you have to stick to a few things that are linked to what the employer values, and you have to nail down what you want them to know early in the letter."

☞ FACT

According to Monster.com, more than 80 percent of job openings are not advertised. A

The purpose of a cover letter is to persuade.

"cold cover letter" can be used to inquire at a company that has not advertised any openings. Cold cover letters, also referred to as uninvited cover letters, are unprompted and can be sent to companies to inquire about possible openings.

READ MORE ABOUT IT: COVER LETTERS AND RESUMES

Beatty, Richard H. *175 High-Impact Cover Letters*. 3d ed. Hoboken, N.J.: Wiley, 2008.

Enelow, Wendy S., and Louise Kursmark. *Cover Letter Magic: Trade Secrets of Professional Resume Writers*. 3d ed. Indianapolis, Ind.: JIST Works, 2006.

Farr, Michael. *The Quick Resume & Cover Letter Book: Write and Use an Effective Resume in Only One Day*. 4th ed. Indianapolis, Ind.: JIST Works, 2007.

Greene, Brenda. *Get the Interview Every Time: Fortune 500 Hiring Professionals' Tips for Writing Winning Resumes and Cover Letters*. New York: Kaplan Business, 2004.

Ireland, Susan. *The Complete Idiot's Guide to the Perfect Resume*. 4th ed. New York: Alpha, 2006.

Kennedy, Joyce Lain. *Cover Letters For Dummies*. Hoboken, N.J.: For Dummies, 2009.

ORGANIZING THE COVER LETTER

One of the most effective methods of writing is called the *pyramid style*. In this type of writing, you place the most important information at the top of the pyramid, or the beginning, and you present it as simply and concisely as possible. You follow this

————. *Resumes For Dummies*. 5th ed. Hoboken, N.J.: For Dummies, 2007.

Noble, David F. *Gallery of Best Cover Letters: Collection of Quality Cover Letters by Professional Resume Writers*. 3d ed. Indianapolis, Ind.: JIST Works, 2007.

Simons, Warren, and Rose Curtis. *The Resume.Com Guide to Writing Unbeatable Resumes*. New York: McGraw-Hill, 2004.

Wallace, Richard. *The Only Resume and Cover Letter Book You'll Ever Need: 600 Resumes for All Industries, 600 Cover Letters for Every Situation, 150 Positions from Entry Level to CEO*. Cincinnati, Ohio: Adams Media, 2008.

Yate, Martin. *Knock 'em Dead Cover Letters: Features the Latest Information on: Online Postings, Email Techniques, and Follow-up Strategies*. 8th ed. Cincinnati, Ohio: Adams Media, 2008.

with the second most important point, the third, the fourth, and so forth. This is the same style that newspaper reporters have used for years to write news articles.

THE PYRAMID STYLE
OF WRITING

In a cover letter, the most important information to include is the position for which you are applying. Otherwise, the reader won't know why you are writing. This information goes in the first

✍ EXERCISE

Write a cover letter. Select a position for which you are qualified based on your work experience and skills. Highlight these skills and experiences and save the cover letter so you can refer to it.

paragraph. You may also wish to include where you heard about the job opening.

The second paragraph should describe the one or two skills or work experiences that make you most qualified for the job. This is where you hook the reader's attention by telling her something she cares about and persuading her to consider you for the position.

A third paragraph might mention several additional but less important qualifications you possess. Conclude the letter by asking for an interview.

BE COMPELLING—THE RESUME

"Employers may get as many as 300 resumes for one job," explains career counselor John Jarvis. "So they have to find a way to narrow them down. Some employers tell me that they put the one-page resumes in one pile, and the two-page resumes go in the trash."

MARIA'S LETTER

328 Cedar Street
Anywhere, USA 09999-9990
January 1, 2009

Ms. Julie Rogers
All-Occasion Clothing Store
10 Prospect Street
Anywhere, USA 09999-0999

Dear Ms. Rogers,

I am applying for the position of assistant manager, which you recently advertised in the Evening Times.

During the past three years, I have worked part time as a sales associate at Calloway and Company, the largest department store in the tri-state area. I was twice voted employee of the month. I received this award in recognition of my service to customers. Calloway and Company also promoted me to assistant manager of my department.

I am graduating in June with an associate's degree in retailing. My grade point average is 3.6, and I have taken courses in marketing and sales as well as in accounting.

I look forward to speaking with you in the near future and discussing what I can contribute to your organization.

Sincerely,

Maria Gonzales

Like the cover letter, the resume persuades an employer to hire you. As Jarvis points out, many employers like a concise resume. In most cases, anything over a page is too long. The resume must also be compelling enough to hook an employer's interest. How do you make it compelling?

Many employers like a concise resume.

Once again, you must start with a clear purpose. This is usually called your "Job Objective." The job objective goes near the top of a resume, so the employer will know immediately what type of job you're seeking.

THE TYPES OF RESUMES

There are several types of resume styles that you can use when applying for a job. These include the chronological, functional, combination, or targeted resume.

A *chronological resume* features a listing of your job experiences in reverse chronological order. (Maria's resume on page 29 is an example of the chronological format.) Your current, or most recent job, is listed first followed by your next most recent job, etc. This is a good resume if you have a strong work history.

A *functional resume* spotlights your skills and experiences instead of your chronological work history. Employment dates are often eliminated in this

(continues)

(continued)

type of resume. This is a good style to use if you have unexplained breaks in your work history or if you are changing jobs.

A *combination resume* features a list of your skills and experiences followed by a chronological record of your employment history. This allows you to both spotlight particular skills that you believe will make you an attractive candidate for employment and provide a more traditional listing of your work experience.

A *targeted resume* specifically lists your skills and experiences that are an exact match for the job position that you are applying for. It begins with a bulleted list of these qualities and then is followed by a chronological listing of employers and job duties you performed that match closely to those required for the new job.

Let's look at Maria's resume, which she developed to accompany her cover letter.

The most compelling type of writing has a clear purpose. In the case of a clear resume, employers know immediately what job you want. Compelling writing is also designed to appeal to your readers. How do you accomplish this on a resume?

MARIA'S RESUME

MARIA GONZALES
328 Cedar Street
Anywhere, USA 09999-9990
(999) 562-3147 (home)
(999) 562-1289 (cell)
mgonzales@anywhere.com (email)

Job Objective   To obtain a position as an
assistant manager in a retail
store

Experience
2006–Present   Calloway and Company
• Worked as sales associate in women's casual
clothing
• Advanced to assistant department manager
• Voted employee of the month three times
• Successfully completed sales-training program

2004–2006   Borders
• Part-time stock clerk
• Trained other clerks

Education
Associate's Degree in Retailing
Central Community College
GPA: 3.6
Courses: marketing, sales, accounting,
economics

Honors graduate, Longwood High School
Vice president of senior class
Member of soccer and tennis teams

Make the resume visually interesting.

One way is to make the resume visually interesting. This means using different kinds of type. For example, Maria puts her headings in boldface type. She also uses bullets to set off key points. However, white space is also important. Your resume should be neat, organized, and original, but not so fancy that it's distracting. If you are applying for a design or creative position, there may be more latitude here.

Don't try to cram too much information on a resume. The resume will look too crowded. Instead, keep it simple.

The resume doesn't get you the job. It gets you the interview. Don't overwhelm them with the resume.

—John Jarvis, career counselor

Remember also to use dynamic words to describe your accomplishments. Always try to use verbs in the *active voice*, not the *passive voice*. "I was given the Employee of the Month Award," uses a passive verb, which sounds weak. Maria presents this information in a stronger way by writing: "Voted employee of the month." Instead of saying "I was appointed assistant department manager," Maria says, "Advanced to assistant department manager." Finally, instead of writing "I was asked to train other clerks," Maria writes, "Trained other clerks."

Descriptive words also make your writing more compelling, and these words can be especially

RESUME KEYWORDS TO AVOID

Hiring managers look at dozens—and sometimes even hundreds—of resumes for a single opening. Many of these resumes feature nice-sounding, but generally empty, words that fail to bring applicant's skills or accomplishments to life. In general, it is better to provide concrete examples of your workplace achievements. Show your accomplishments, rather than use generic words that leave the hiring manager cold when reading your resume. CareerBuilder.com advises job applicants to avoid the following words on resumes when possible:

- Aggressive
- Ambitious
- Competent
- Creative
- Detail-oriented
- Determined
- Efficient
- Experienced
- Flexible
- Goal-oriented
- Hard-working
- Independent
- Innovative
- Knowledgeable
- Logical
- Motivated
- Meticulous
- People person
- Professional
- Reliable
- Resourceful
- Self-motivated
- Successful
- Team player
- Well-organized

powerful on a resume. Don't exaggerate what you have accomplished, but use descriptive words to bring it to life. Instead of saying, "completed a training course," Maria writes, "Successfully completed sales-training program." If you are a "fully experienced" stock clerk, say so. If you have "extensive knowledge" of computers, include that information as well. These simple descriptive words stand out on the page and attract the reader's attention.

Chris Hanson is applying for a part-time job after school. He wants to be an animal handler or kennel worker. Chris has worked part time for three years at the local Audubon Society. He has valuable experience caring for sick and injured animals. He also trained other volunteers to care for the animals. Before this, Chris volunteered at a local nature center. He completed a training course in how to conduct

✍ EXERCISE

- Use the information about Chris to develop a resume that he can use to find a job.

- Write a resume for yourself. It should reflect the cover letter you wrote in the preceding exercise. It should be detailed and accurate—busy employers do not have patience for typos.

SURF THE WEB: COVER LETTERS AND RESUMES

About.com: Job Searching: Resumes, Cover Letters, and Employment-Related Letters
http://jobsearch.about.com/od/resumes/u/resumesandletters.htm

CareerOneStop: Resumes and Interviews
http://www.jobbankinfo.org

CollegeGrad.com: Resumes
http://www.collegegrad.com/resume

JobStar Central: Resumes
http://www.jobstar.org/tools/resume

Monster Career Advice: Resume & Letters
http://career-advice.monster.com/resume-tips/home.aspx

The Riley Guide: Resumes & Cover Letters
http://www.rileyguide.com/letters.html

Vault.com: Resumes and Advice
http://www.vault.com/index.jsp

tours of the center. Every Saturday, he conducted tours for up to 50 adults and children. Currently, Chris is attending high school, where he writes for the newspaper and maintains a 3.2 GPA.

BE CLEAR—MEMOS AND REPORTS

Good writing is simple and clear. You should leave no doubt in the minds of your readers about what you are trying to say to them. Unfortunately, some people seem to forget this principle, especially when they write.

A task force from the National Council of Teachers of English and the International Reading Association tried to develop national standards on how to write English. They came up with 12 basic rules. Rule 5 states "Students employ a wide range of strategies as they write and use different writing process elements appropriately to communicate with different audiences for a variety of purposes." What is a process element? What does the panel mean by "communicate with different audiences for a variety of purposes?" These terms are so vague that no one could be sure. The *New York Times* wrote that the rules were written in "a tongue barely recognizable as English." And they were written by English teachers!

"Unclear, poorly written, or confusing" is the verdict of vice presidents of two hundred major U.S. companies on a full third of the business writing they confront.

—**Kenneth Roman and Joel Raphaelson**
in *Writing That Works: How to Communicate Effectively in Business*

Avoid Big, Fancy Words

Some writers seem to think that you need big, fancy-sounding words to lend importance to a subject. Too often, these words make the subject far more complicated than it needs to be. Even worse, your readers may not understand what you mean.

Jason works in an office. His supervisor asked him to write a brief memo and post it in the coffee room. Here's what Jason wrote:

TO: All Employees
FM: Supervisor
SUBJ: Refreshments

The experimental process of making available a variety of liquid refreshments on the honor system is undergoing reconsideration. In the event that employees who appropriate these refreshments without leaving the proper remuneration do not terminate these activities, the refreshments will be eliminated in the future.

Jason used a lot of long and complicated words because he was trying to sound important. After all, he had been asked to write this memo by his supervisor. But the meaning of what Jason was saying was not very clear. He really could have written it very simply: "If employees don't pay for refreshments we will no longer offer refreshments on the honor system."

Choose words that are easy to pronounce and can be understood by everyone. Unfamiliar words

One sure way to stop readers cold in their tracks is to write long, involved sentences that are difficult to follow.

cause readers to slow down or even stop reading all together. You don't want your readers to stop reading; they will lose the message that you are trying to communicate.

One sure way to stop readers cold in their tracks is to write long, involved sentences that are difficult to follow. Cheryl's supervisor asked her to write a brief report on the training program she attended at the restaurant where she worked. She began the report this way:

> The training program, whose interesting classes, excellent instruction, and extensive hands-on experience, afforded me a unique glimpse at different types of jobs in our organization, and it, right from the start of the program and the very first class which I attended more than two weeks ago, gave me the chance to meet some of the people with whom I will be working in the future, since they were in my training classes.

This sentence is 73 words long. If you try to read it aloud, it will leave you completely out of breath. Since there are several important ideas in the sentence—why the training program was effective, what Cheryl learned, and whom she met—they could easily be presented as separate sentences.

Cheryl's sentence also has other problems. Sentences are easy to understand when the subjects and verbs are close together: "She writes a report." But Cheryl separates her subjects and verbs by long clauses. In the first part of the sentence, the subject "program" is separated from the verb "afforded." In the second part of the sentence, the subject "it" is also separated by a long clause from the verb "gave." This makes her writing hard to follow. Cheryl also uses more words than she needs to communicate her ideas. The sentence might be rewritten this way:

> The training program featured interesting classes, excellent instruction, and extensive hands-on experience. It taught me about many types of jobs. I also had a chance to meet some of the people who will be working with me.

In business writing, a good rule of thumb is to keep the sentences as easy to understand as possible. If you have two important ideas to present, use two separate sentences. Eliminate all unnecessary words.

BE CORRECT—ALL OF THE TIME

Career counselor John Jarvis explains what one employer was looking for in the position of administrative assistant. "He emphasized communication skills," Jarvis said. "He didn't want to waste time proofing the administrative assistant's work. He wanted to dictate the letter, and expected his assis-

✍ EXERCISE

Rewrite the following sentences to make them clearer and simpler.

• Greenway Tree Farms, because of the strong price for Christmas trees, a larger demand for trees expected during the holiday season, and the improving economy in the eastern and southern regions of the country, will probably experience continued growth in the fourth quarter.

• Our sales representatives, since they may be new employees in our firm and are not always informed about the products that they are supposed to be describing to our customers, may sound embarrassed and confused and, even worse, cause confusion in the minds of the customers.

Have you rewritten the sentences above to make them more concise? If so, compare your rewrites with the ones below. Remember that there are many ways to make confusing sentences more coherent.

• Greenway Tree Farms will continue to experience growth in the fourth quarter. Growth will be fueled by increasing demand for trees during the holiday season, rising prices for trees, and an improving economy in the eastern and southeastern United States.

• New sales representatives may not always be able to describe our products to customers. This situation must be remedied because this lack of knowledge may cause confusion among our customers.

tant to punctuate it correctly and use proper spelling and capitalization."

The workplace is different from school. In your classes, Bs and Cs may be acceptable. Your teachers will allow you to make a few mistakes. On the job, mistakes lessen the impact of your writing. A misspelled word, a comma in the wrong place, a period where there should be a question mark—all of these mistakes distract the reader from what you're trying

COMMUNICATION FACTS

- According to experts, people often confuse communication with persuasion. Communication is the transmission of messages among people or groups; persuasion is a person or group's deliberate attempt to make another person or group adopt a certain idea, belief, or action.

- Expressing differences is a vital part of workplace communication, as long as you avoid an accusatory tone when doing so.

- Jackie Sloane, president of Sloane Communications, offered the following advice in the *Chicago Tribune*: "If you're having a challenging encounter with the boss, ask yourself, 'What does my boss want? What might he/she be terrified about?' "

SOUND-ALIKE AND LOOK-ALIKE WORDS

Accept	receive	Except	exclude
Affect	influence (verb)	Effect	result (noun), bring about
Complement	something that completes	Compliment	praise
Desert	dry landscape	Dessert	last course of a meal
Eminent	famous	Imminent	about to happen
Foreword	introduction to a book	Forward	ahead; toward the front
Allusion	an implied reference	Illusion	a false impression
Precede	to come before	Proceed	to come from a source or to move on from something
Principal	person who runs a school	Principle	a truth or value
Stationary	in a fixed position	Stationery	writing paper
Tacked	to add on or attach	Tact	sensitivity to another's feelings
Tic	an involuntary spasm; twitching	Tick	the sound of a clock; a tiny insect
Toe	appendages of the foot	Tow	the act of pulling
Trade-in	(noun) an exchange	Trade in	(verb) to buy or sell goods
Undo	to reverse	Undue	excessive

to say. They tell the reader that your writing, and perhaps your thinking, is sloppy and unorganized.

Now that most writers use a computer, they rely on spell-check to catch those misspelled words. But spell-check can take you only so far. It will correct misspellings, but it will not tell you if you're using the wrong word in a specific situation. One computer consulting firm submitted a proposal to a large landscaping company to upgrade their computer system. The proposal was designed to be a "turnkey" operation, which meant that all the hardware and software would be installed. And the system would be ready to use. Instead of "turnkey," the proposal said "turkey" operation. Spell-check did not catch this mistake, because "turkey" is a word, just like "turnkey." No one had bothered to proofread the proposal adequately.

Sometimes we may use the wrong word in a situation. The following table provides a list of sound-alike and look-alike words that give many writers trouble. Of course, there are others, too. If you have a question about which word to use in a specific sentence, look up the word in a dictionary.

Whenever you write, you must proofread your document carefully before sending it to a reader. Here are three proofreading rules that may be helpful to you:

- Don't proofread on the computer—it's too hard to spot mistakes on a screen. Instead, make a hard copy and proof it at your desk.

- Don't proofread immediately after you've finished writing. You're too close to the project, and you won't see the mistakes easily. Instead, put the writing away for a day or two; then proofread it.

- Proofread three times: once for content, clarity, and conciseness, once for grammar and punctuation, and once to make sure you've used the right words.

IMPROVE YOUR COMMUNICATION SKILLS

In order to communicate well, you need to be able to effectively proofread your memos, emails, reports, and other correspondence. But proofreading involves a lot more than just scanning a document over and over until you find an error. In addition to checking a document's content, clarity, and conciseness, you have to make sure that you have used proper punctuation and grammar. To help get you started, here are a few of the reference materials professional editors and writers use to make sure that their work is perfect:

Cappon, Rene J. *The Associated Press Guide to Punctuation*. New York: Basic Books, 2003.

Shertzer, Margaret. *The Elements of Grammar*. Reading, Mass.: Longman, 1996.

Strunk, William Jr., and E. B. White. *The Elements of Style*. 4th ed. Boston: Allyn & Beacon, 2000.

THE PITFALLS OF EMAIL

Many of the problems that afflict writing are now showing up in electronic mail. Email has become an effective way of sending memos and other types of communication that must arrive quickly. "I receive email all the time," reports freelance artist Richard Rossiter, who designs book covers. "But the mistakes, the misspellings are appalling. No one takes any time to write anything."

University of Chicago. *The Chicago Manual of Style: The Essential Guide for Writers, Editors, and Publishers.* 15th ed. Chicago: The University of Chicago Press, 2003.

Additionally, here are some publications that are geared toward the general public:

Anderson, Laura Killen. *McGraw-Hill's Proofreading Handbook.* 2d ed. New York: McGraw-Hill, 2006.

Gilad, Suzanne. *Copyediting & Proofreading For Dummies.* Hoboken, N.J.: For Dummies, 2007.

Truss, Lynne. *Eats, Shoots & Leaves: The Zero Tolerance Approach to Punctuation.* New York: Gotham Books, 2006.

Walsh, Bill. *The Elephants of Style: A Trunkload of Tips on the Big Issues and Gray Areas of Contemporary American English.* New York: McGraw-Hill, 2004.

Simple and familiar words have power.

Email is subject to the same rules that govern other types of writing. That is, the writing should be clear and concise. Information should be presented in a compelling manner, with no mistakes in grammar, punctuation, or spelling. The purpose of the communication should be clearly stated, and it should be delivered in a way that appeals to the reader.

In their book, *The Elements of Email Style: Communicate Effectively via Electronic Mail,* David Angell and Brent Heslop explain that information should be presented in short, coherent units. Readers, they say, are "turned off by large chunks of text." They also urge you to keep your language simple. "If a word confuses your readers and sends them scurrying for the dictionary, it has broken their concentration," Angell and Heslop explain. "Simple and familiar words have power."

If these basic tips haven't provided you with enough guidance, here are a few more to help you create professional emails:

- *Always edit before you hit "send."* Take the time to proofread and edit your emails to ensure that you have used good grammar, punctuation, and spelling. A well-written email will make your boss's or customer's life easier.

- *Use email only when appropriate.* Although a survey of workers by OfficeTeam found that email is the preferred form of business communication, it is not always the most

PREFERRED METHODS OF BUSINESS COMMUNICATION, 2007

Email	65 percent
Face-to-face meeting	31 percent
Paper memo	3 percent
Voice mail	1 percent

Source: OfficeTeam

appropriate communication method. Sometimes a face-to-face meeting or phone call might be a better approach—especially when dealing with sensitive or emotional topics.

- *Don't forget to include a subject line.* Including a subject line that briefly summarizes the purpose of your email will save the recipient valuable time.

- *Keep it brief.* Remember that your boss or coworkers receive dozens, if not hundreds, of emails a day. Use the pyramid style of writing to keep your emails short and to the point.

- *Avoid using emoticons.* They are inappropriate in business settings.

THE 10 COMMANDMENTS OF GOOD WRITING

1. I realize that all good writing must have a clear purpose.

2. I recognize that less is more—too many words can bore my reader.

3. I understand that the most important information belongs at the beginning of my document.

4. I avoid all mistakes in grammar, punctuation, and spelling.

5. I think about what my readers want before beginning to write.

6. I make an impact on my readers by making my writing powerful.

7. I don't use complex words when I can use simple ones.

8. I leave out all information that does not relate to my main purpose.

9. I use descriptive words to bring my writing to life.

10. I never assume that my readers know more than they do.

- *Avoid using abbreviations and slang.*
  Unless the recipient is familiar with
  an abbreviation, its use will just be
  confusing and slow communication.
  Additionally, email slang (such as CU
  and GR8) is inappropriate in workplace
  communications.

- *Never reply to an email in anger.* Unlike
  face-to-face communication, it is easy
  to misconstrue the tone of an email.
  Completely innocuous comments or jokes
  can be taken the wrong way. If you receive
  an email that makes you angry or confused,
  take a deep breath, and wait to cool off
  before you reply. Or better yet, talk to
  the individual face-to-face to address any
  confusion.

☛ FACT

The average person in the United States reads at
a seventh- or eighth-grade level.

✔ TRUE OR FALSE: ANSWERS

Do You Know How to Write with a Purpose?

1. When writing for others, it's important to
know your reader.

True. Every document needs to be crafted with the end reader in mind—whether it is your boss (who might just want the quick facts), your coworker (who might need a detailed update about the project), or a customer (who just wants to know when the project will be completed and how much it will cost).

2. There are three keys, known as the 3 Cs, to a successful resume: concise, clear, and correct.

Partially true. There are actually 4 Cs. A successful resume is concise, compelling, clear, and correct. Many people can craft a concise, clear, and correct document, but if you don't make your resume compelling, it might not stand out. Remember, hiring managers may receive hundreds of resumes for a single position! How do you make your resume compelling? By making it visually interesting (a combination of interesting fonts, bullet points, and just enough white space) and including descriptive details about your abilities rather than empty words that may sound good but don't really convey your talents and qualifications.

3. Cover letters can be up to two pages in length.

False. Hiring managers are swamped with resumes, and sending a two-page cover letter is a sure path to the trash can. Write a concise

✍ EXERCISE

- Find examples of writing from magazines and newspapers that you admire. Notice how they try to excite the reader's interest and present main points. Make a file of powerful writing and refer to it to help with your own writing.

- Write the first paragraph of a letter, asking people to donate their time or an item to a bake sale. The bake sale is designed to raise money for charity. Make sure the paragraph appeals to the reader and utilizes the 4 Cs of good writing.

- Start a blog on the Internet. Write about your own life or focus on one of your hobbies or interests—such as the environment, basketball, video games, or politics. While writing in your own voice is important when crafting your blog, be sure to follow The 10 Commandments of Good Writing on page 47. If you don't know how to start, visit https://www.blogger.com/start for more information.

cover letter by detailing only what the reader will find most persuasive to help you land the job.

4. It's okay for business emails to have typos and be full of slang.

False. Would you use poor grammar and talk in slang on the phone or in a face-to-face meeting with your boss or a customer? Definitely no! Business emails should contain excellent grammar, proper punctuation, and be professionally written in every way.

IN SUMMARY . . .

- Define the purpose of your writing in a few summary sentences.

- Find out who your readers are, what they need to know, what their attitudes are, and why they should care.

- Implement the 4 Cs into your writing:
  Compelling
  Concise
  Clear
  Correct

- Write a short and clear cover letter that highlights your experience and skills and tells the employer why you are a good candidate for the job.

- Create a detailed, professional-looking resume in order to get a job interview.

- Emails should be composed using the same rules that other types of writing follow. Present your information in short chunks; large chunks of text do not appeal to readers.

2

SPEAKING WITH CONFIDENCE

J im was a head counselor at Camp Sunrise. On Awards Day at the end of the season, he was expected to stand up and speak to the large group of campers and their parents. Jim had prepared his talk and even memorized what he wanted to say. But as he sat on the stage waiting to be introduced, he became nervous. He had been dreading this moment for days.

Finally, Jim's name was called. He stood up and walked slowly to the podium. As he moved to center stage, his legs felt wobbly. His palms were sweaty and his stomach started doing flip-flops. Jim looked out at all those faces. Suddenly, he wished he could disappear.

"Thank you for coming here today," he began in a tense, high-pitched voice. "It's been a wonderful opportunity to work with so many great campers this summer. Now I'd like to tell you a story about one of them."

DID YOU KNOW?

Employers surveyed in 2007 by OfficeTeam rated verbal communication skills as the second most important soft skill in demand among administrative staff at their companies. The ability to write for business ranked sixth.

Source: *Fitting In, Standing Out and Building Remarkable Work Teams*

✔ TRUE OR FALSE?

Do You Know How to Speak with Confidence?

1. I don't need to be a good public speaker. Public speaking is just for politicians and newscasters.

2. To give a successful speech, you need to do a lot of research and practice.

3. Most speeches will work for any demographic group.

4. The 3 Ts of successful public speaking are: (1) Tell the audience what you're going to say at the beginning of the talk; (2) Tell the audience what you're going to say to them in the body of the talk; and (3) Tell the audience what you told them in the conclusion.

Test yourself as you read through this chapter. The answers appear on pages 77–79.

All eyes were on him. Everyone seemed to be waiting for him to begin the story. They waited . . . and waited . . . and waited. Jim's mind had suddenly gone blank. He couldn't remember what he wanted to say.

"I knew it yesterday," he thought. "Why can't I remember it now? Why?" It seemed like an hour had passed. But in reality it was only 30 seconds. Panic seized him. Jim knew everyone was staring at him. And he just wanted to get out of there. He could stand it no longer. Jim turned from the audience and fled the stage.

THE IMPORTANCE OF PUBLIC SPEAKING

The ability to deliver an effective talk is one of the most valuable skills you can possess. If you want to be a leader in school, public speaking is often essential. As a class officer, head of the student council, or president of a club, you are often called on to stand up and speak to a group. Public speaking is also important in the workplace. As career counselor Rozeanne Burt explains, "The people who can stand up and give a talk stand out and are set apart from other employees."

Yet most people are afraid of public speaking. In fact, recent polls indicate that they fear it more than death itself.

Stage fright is not uncommon, even among good speakers. But they generally don't react the way Jim

Public speaking is a very important workplace skill. You may often be required to present information and your ideas to your managers and coworkers. (Jose Luis Pelaez Inc., Corbis)

did. Instead, there are several approaches they use to conquer their fears.

ENLIST THE AID OF THE AUDIENCE

Remember, the people in the audience genuinely want you to succeed. They've come to hear you speak. They want to know what you have to say to them. They may be experts on the subject of your talk or they may know nothing about it; regardless, they want to hear what you have to say about it.

TOP 10 FEARS AMONG AMERICANS

1. Public speaking
2. Heights
3. Insects
4. Financial trouble
5. Deep water
6. Sickness
7. Death
8. Flying
9. Loneliness
10. Dogs

Make eye contact with an individual in the audience who is a friend or acquaintance. As you begin to talk, speak only to that individual. Or if you don't know anyone in the audience, pretend you are just sharing information with a friend. By turning a speech into a one-on-one conversation, it will seem less intimidating.

If you are still nervous when it's time to deliver the speech, take a deep breath and remind yourself that you don't have to be so serious. Imagining the audience in their underwear usually helps people lighten up and put speeches into perspective.

The people in the audience genuinely want you to succeed.

MAKE YOUR STAGE FRIGHT WORK FOR YOU

Fear requires a lot of energy. Instead of letting the fear undermine your talk, channel this energy in other directions. For example, using gestures to reinforce the main points of your talk can make it more dynamic. Communications consultant Richard Southern advises that you "get your body involved in what you're saying." This will add power to your presentation and keep your audience involved from beginning to end.

Try to think of stage fright in a positive way. Fear is your friend. It makes your reflexes sharper. It heightens your energy, adds a sparkle to your eye, and color to your cheeks. When you are nervous about speaking you are more conscious of your posture and breathing. With all those good side effects you will actually look healthier and more attractive.

—Tom Antion, author of the article "Learn How to Be a Professional Speaker"

BE PREPARED

In his book, *Inspire Any Audience*, Tony Jeary explains that one way to overcome pre-speech jitters is to "know what you're talking about. Thorough preparation equals total confidence," he says. Some speak-

STAGE FRIGHT

You know that stage fright is setting in if you have the following:

- Dry mouth
- Sweaty or cold hands
- Rapid pulse
- Tight throat
- Nervous or upset stomach
- Shaky lips, knees, or hands

ers try "winging it" and hope for the best. But they often fall flat on their faces and fail to impress the audience. Preparation is the key to successful public speaking.

Prepare to communicate with your audience by researching your topic. Books, magazines, journals, newspapers, the Internet, and advocacy groups are all helpful. Government sources and legal sources can also provide you with a lot of credible information and statistics.

It takes three weeks to prepare a good ad-lib speech.

—**Mark Twain, American writer**

Create a rough outline of what you want to communicate to the audience. Additions and changes will likely be made to the outline, but it is good to have an organized start so you have some direction and you don't leave important information out.

DID YOU KNOW?

- The fear of public speaking is known as glossophobia.

- Approximately 75 percent of people have a fear of speaking in public.

- Speech anxiety affects about the same percentages of women and men, although men are more apt to seek treatment to address their fear.

Source: Speech Topics Help, Advice & Ideas

Melissa had to deliver a brief talk about her part-time job at the print shop. She began by explaining how she uses desktop publishing to design brochures. Then she described the process she followed to get her job in the first place. Melissa spoke about her boss and her coworkers. Next, she discussed some of the interesting projects she completed for customers. Then she included something she forgot to say about desktop publishing. Finally, Melissa thanked her audience and sat down.

Melissa had spent very little time preparing her presentation. It had no central purpose.

Consequently, it made little sense to her listeners. Unfortunately, many presentations sound the same way. It is not uncommon for people to sit through a presentation and find themselves wondering what they're supposed to get out of it. For this reason, it's important to make your purpose known.

In Chapter 1, we talk about the summary sentences that define the purpose of your writing. Similarly, the first step in preparing any good talk is to develop summary sentences that clearly define the purpose of your presentation.

☛ FACT

In the United States, an estimated 80,000 people stand up and speak before an audience every day.

Some speakers confuse the subject with the purpose of their talk. The *subject* is usually quite broad. For instance, your boss might ask you to speak about the training course on computers that you just completed. With a subject that broad, you could say a great many things about it. A good talk, however, usually has a sharply focused *purpose* or something specific you want to say about your subject. Listeners get overwhelmed if you try to tell them too much. The summary sentences define that purpose. They remind you and enable your listeners to know why you are speaking.

SAMPLE SUMMARY SENTENCES

Subject
The computer training course

Purpose
To explain how the course will help me on my job. My talk will give three examples of how I expect to use what I learned.

Subject
My volunteer work at the homeless shelter

Purpose
To persuade other students to volunteer at the center. My talk will point out how this work benefits the homeless and how students can derive fulfillment from it.

Subject
My woodworking hobby

Purpose
To describe the process of making an item out of wood. My talk will discuss the important steps to follow.

UNDERSTANDING YOUR AUDIENCE

Crystal had been asked to speak to a group of customers who were taking a tour of her plant. She was

✍ EXERCISE

1. For each of the following topics, develop a purpose for a talk. Write the purpose in summary sentences.

   - A recent vacation

   - An especially difficult homework assignment

   - A part-time job after school

   - A skill you learned

   - A person who has influenced you

2. Write a speech about a new solar-powered car for several audiences. How would the tone, content, and overall presentation vary for an eight-grade class, a car club, scientists, and potential customers?

supposed to talk about the area where she and the other members of her team worked.

"What will I say?" Crystal wondered. "I've never given a talk like this before." Finally, she decided to discuss it with her supervisor.

"They're not technicians, like you are," Ms. Muniz, her supervisor, explained. "They don't need to know all the details of the manufacturing process."

The most important step in preparing any presentation is to understand your audience.

"That's right; they're customers, aren't they?" Crystal said. "They want to be sure we're manufacturing quality products."

"Exactly," Ms. Muniz agreed. "So briefly describe how you carry out our quality process."

Chapter 1 discusses the importance of "writing for your reader." The same principle applies to public speaking. The most important step in preparing any presentation is to understand your audience. "Before you start," advises Donald Walton in his book *Are You Communicating?*, "it's wise to reflect on who your audience will be and what their primary interests are."

LISTENER ANALYSIS

As you prepare a talk, conduct a *listener analysis*—analyze the people who are going to receive your talk. This is similar to what you'd do before starting to write a memo or report. This information will help you determine what to say.

Ask yourself the following questions:

- *What do my listeners want to know?* If you don't provide information that interests them, you'll put them to sleep. Find out what they care about and cover this material in your talk.

- *How much do they already know?* They may be experts or they may know almost nothing about your topic. You don't want to "talk down" to your listeners. But you also don't want to speak over their heads. Determine what your audience knows and pitch your talk to your audience's level of understanding.

READ MORE ABOUT IT: PUBLIC SPEAKING

Bell, Arthur H. *Butterflies Be Gone: An 8-Step Approach to Sweat-Proof Public Speaking.* New York: McGraw-Hill, 2008.

Benjamin, Susan J. *Speak with Success: A Student's Step-by-Step Guide to Fearless Public Speaking.* Tucson, Ariz.: Good Year Books, 2007.

Kushner, Malcolm. *Public Speaking For Dummies.* 2d ed. Hoboken, N.J.: For Dummies, 2004.

Macinnis, J. Lyman. *The Elements of Great Public Speaking: How to Be Calm, Confident, and Compelling.* Berkeley, Calif.: Ten Speed Press, 2006.

Maxey, Cyndi, and Kevin E. O'Connor. *Speak Up!: A Woman's Guide to Presenting Like a Pro.* New York: St. Martin's Griffin, 2008.

Zeoli, Richard. *The 7 Principles of Public Speaking: Proven Methods from a PR Professional.* New York: Skyhorse Publishing, 2008.

- *Where do they stand?* Your listeners may be likely to agree with what you're saying, or they may need a lot of convincing. Find out their attitudes; then determine what to say to persuade them of your point of view.

THE 3 TS

One of the best ways of organizing any presentation is also the simplest. It's called the 3 Ts, which are as follows:

1. Tell the audience what you're going to say at the beginning of the talk.

2. Tell the audience what you're going to say to them in the body of the talk.

3. Tell the audience what you told them in the conclusion.

Let's explain this further.

Many speakers simply launch into a presentation without ever explaining their purpose for speaking. They expect the audience to figure it out. Frequently, the audience doesn't or won't figure it out, and they quickly lose interest.

☞ FACT

The attention span of most adults is about seven minutes.

At the beginning of your presentation, you should explain your purpose for speaking. This tells the audience why you are talking to them. You can almost literally present your summary sentences. "I want to explain how my computer-training course will help me on the job. I'll give you three examples of how I expect to use what I learned." Now your listeners know what to expect. You won't lose their attention.

In the auction industry, where your microphone is an essential tool, it makes sense that communication skills would be vital assets. Not only do you need to be able to clearly communicate over the mic, but you also need to be able to effectively communicate with your buyers, sellers, and employees. It's important to know what your buyers and sellers expect out of the auction, and the only way to gain that knowledge is to communicate with both parties. You also want to keep your auctions running smoothly, and this requires constant communication with your employees. Last but not least, you need to be able to communicate with other auctioneers, through organizations like the National Auctioneers Association, to gain the latest insight on educational, technological, and networking opportunities across the country. My experience as an international champion auctioneer has taught me that you need to effectively communicate to succeed.

—Jodi Sweeney, Sweeney Auction Service

During the body of the talk, mention your summary sentences again as you cover each topic. At the conclusion, you can repeat another version of the summary sentences. "As you can see, the course was extremely helpful. The three examples I've just discussed show you how I intend to use the course." This leaves the purpose of your talk firmly fixed in the minds of your listeners.

HOOK THE AUDIENCE

The 3 Ts provide a structure for your presentation. However, structure alone doesn't bring a presentation to life. Before you present your summary statements and details of your speech, you need to grab your audience's attention with a good opening. This same tactic is used in many types of media. In television, for example, producers like to present a *teaser* before a program begins. This is something that hooks the viewers so they will keep watching. If it's a sitcom, the teaser may be a very funny scene from the story. If it's an adventure series, the teaser may be several action scenes from the show. Producers know that if viewers aren't hooked quickly, they may decide to channel surf.

Your audience is the same way. You have to hook their attention very quickly or they may tune out.

Stories and anecdotes have proven to be good openings. A startling piece of information or a newspaper headline is also an attention grabber. Your opening should be something that will grab the interest of your listeners, but it must also be something directly related to your purpose for speaking.

You can never be a great presenter without understanding and mastering strong openings.

—**Frank Paolo** in *How to Make a Great Presentation in 2 Hours*

Gerald is the assistant manager of an electronics store in a shopping mall. He began a talk to his employees this way:

Recently, I went to a store to buy some in-line skates. After looking at several varieties, I had a few questions. I waited for a salesperson to come over and help me. There were very few people in the store, but I noticed that none of the three salespeople tried to help any of them. They stood in a corner talking to each other. Finally, I went over to see if I could get some help.

"Excuse me," I said. "Could you answer some questions for me about your in-line skates?" One of the salespeople glared at me. "Look, you're interrupting an important discussion here," she said. "Don't be in such a hurry. We'll get to you in a few minutes."

Well, I wasn't about to wait until she was ready. I turned around and walked out of the store.

I'm telling you this story because it illustrates the purpose of my talk today: If we don't want to lose customers, we must learn how to satisfy them. And I want to explain how we do that.

Gerald began his talk with a personal anecdote that was closely tied to his purpose. The anecdote hooked his listeners. Then he could make an easy transition to his summary sentences. Gerald also might have started his presentation this way:

According to a recent survey, 53 percent of consumers said they would be shopping less this year, and 30 percent said they expect to spend less money shopping. What this means for us is that we have to do everything possible to hold on to our customers. To do that, we must always try to satisfy them. And in this talk I want to explain how we do that.

In this case, Gerald opened with a startling statistic that no one had probably heard before. Then he tied it directly to the purpose of his presentation.

OPEN WITH A JOKE?

Carol was giving a talk at parents' night in her school. She decided to begin with a joke—one that most of her friends found very funny. Unfortunately, she forgot that an audience of adults might be quite different from a group of her friends. As she completed the joke, Carol waited for everyone to laugh. Instead, there was stony silence. No one in the audience reacted. The joke had been a complete dud. Even worse, Carol had made a negative impression right from the beginning of her talk. As a result, no one in the audience was inclined to listen very closely to the rest of what she was saying.

☞ FACT

The Internet is an excellent place to find anecdotes on everything from wax museums to medical bloopers. Try anecdotage.com (http://www.anecdotage.com), which labels itself as the site with anecdotes from acrobats to zippers and zoos.

"Humor is very high risk and I don't recommend it," explains communications consultant Granville Toogood. "When an early joke goes flat, it tends to take all the bubbles out of whatever follows." For years, speakers opened their talks with a joke. But for many of them, it proved deadly. Sometimes the speaker wasn't a good storyteller. Or, as in Carol's case, her idea of what was funny wasn't the same as her audience's. Opening with an anecdote, an example, or an interesting fact is usually much more effective.

✍ EXERCISE

Using one of the topics from the previous exercise, write a hook to open your talk. Practice reading multiple opening lines to a friend and decide which is the most compelling. Remember, a good opening is the only way to get the audience interested, so it is worth it to put in some time finding a solid opener.

THE BENEFITS OF HUMOR

Although it is risky, humor is an effective tool if you can perfect it. Humor does many things. It

- relaxes the audience.
- makes your speech more enjoyable.
- negates any hostility that may be present.
- overcomes introductions that may be overly flattering.
- lets the audience know that you don't take yourself too seriously.
- lightens up a dry subject.

If you decide to incorporate humor into a speech, be sure to do the following:

- *Know your audience.* A joke that may seem funny to people in your age group may not seem as humorous to people who are your parents' age or may even fall flat with people who are your grandparents' age.

- *Be conservative when using humor.* Avoid the outlandish and sarcastic; try to find humor that appeals to every demographic group in your audience.

- *Use humor only if you're used to doing so.* If you are a naturally humorous person in your daily life, than it might be okay to try a little humor in a speech. If you are a more fact-based, serious person, it is better to stay in your comfort zone and avoid using humor in your presentations.

- *Make it relevant.* Any humor you use should relate directly to the topic of your speech.

- *Rehearse.* Practice and memorize your humorous story or joke in order to be fully engaged with the audience and appear spontaneous (even if you spent hours the night before practicing your speech).

- *Never use foul or profane language during a speech.*

COMPLETING YOUR PRESENTATION

The best talks should be concise as well as compelling.

Talks don't have to be long to be effective. Lincoln's Gettysburg Address is a perfect example—it is perhaps the most memorable speech ever delivered by an American leader, and it only lasted a few minutes. The best talks should be concise as well as compelling. This means that the body, like the introduction, should contain interesting anecdotes and examples. These things help bring your ideas to life and hold the attention of your audience. But always make sure that any information you present strengthens the purpose of your talk and supports your summary sentences.

You don't have to write thousands of words to effectively communicate. President Lincoln's Gettysburg Address was not lengthy, but it is considered one of the most memorable speeches ever made. (AP Photo)

SURF THE WEB:
USING HUMOR IN SPEECHES

The Art of Using Humor in Public
http://www.squaresail.com/auh.html

How to Use Humor in Public Speaking
http://www.expertvillage.com/video/5830_public-speaking-humor.htm

Humor in Public Speaking
http://www.msstate.edu/org/toastmasters/resources/humor_in_speaking.pdf

Public Speaking Expert: Using Humour in a Speech
http://www.publicspeakingexpert.co.uk/UsingHumourInASpeech.html

Finally, repeat your purpose at the close of your talk. And if you can, illustrate it with an interesting story from your own experience or from something you've read. The more concrete and specific you can make a talk, the more likely your audience is to remember it.

☛ FACT

Lincoln's Gettysburg Address is only 268 words long.

PRACTICE MAKES (ALMOST) PERFECT

Creating a successful speech takes time. It involves developing a clear purpose, analyzing your audience, creating a structure for your talk, and bringing it to life with interesting information. Once you

THE EIGHT SECRETS OF SUCCESSFUL SPEAKING

1. Define the purpose of your presentation before doing anything else.

2. Spend plenty of time preparing your talk so it will be effective.

3. Hook the attention of your listeners early in a speech so they will listen to the rest of it.

4. Tell the audience why you're speaking to them at the beginning, the middle, and the end of your talk.

5. Overcome stage fright by making it work for you.

6. Use stories and anecdotes to bring your talk to life.

7. Evaluate each talk you give so you can constantly improve your skills.

8. Never stop practicing.

✍ EXERCISE

Complete the talk you were developing in the previous exercise.

- Construct an interesting opening to your talk, which hooks the audience and relates to your summary sentences.
- Make three main points in the body.
- Support those points with examples, interesting facts, or anecdotes.
- Create a conclusion that repeats the purpose of your presentation.

have prepared the talk, put the key points on a few note cards. Then rehearse it several times. This will enable you to become comfortable with the talk and improve your delivery. Preparation and practice will make you a better speaker.

✔ TRUE OR FALSE: ANSWERS

Do You Know How to Speak with Confidence?

1. I don't need to be a good public speaker. Public speaking is just for politicians and newscasters.

False. Employers surveyed in 2007 by the National Association of Colleges and Employers ranked communication skills as very-to-extremely important for job candidates. So, if you want a job, you will need to hone your public-speaking skills.

2. To give a successful speech, you need to do a lot of research and practice.

True. Effective public speakers can make a speech look effortless, but don't be deceived. To be a successful speaker, you need to spend hours researching your topic and then practice your speech until you have mastered it.

3. Most speeches will work for any demographic group.

False. Would you give the same speech extolling the virtues of your Wii to a group of fellow gamers and to a group that has never used the game console? Definitely not. A good speech provides information that is carefully researched and presented for a particular audience.

4. The 3 Ts of successful public speaking are: (1) Tell the audience what you're going to say at the beginning of the talk; (2) Tell the audience what you're going to say to them in the body of the talk; and (3) Tell the audience what you told them in the conclusion.

True. You want to keep your audience focused and interested. The best way to do this is by detailing what you're going to cover in the speech and how it will benefit them.

IN SUMMARY . . .

- Although public speaking can be intimidating, keep in mind that the people in the audience want you to succeed.

- Know the subject and the purpose of the speech you are going to give. Your speech and your summary sentences should be focused mainly on the purpose.

- Open your speech by hooking the audience with an interesting anecdote, statistic, or joke.

- Conduct a listener analysis before you deliver a speech. Find out what the audience wants to know about, how much they already know, and what their attitudes are.

- Instead of letting stage fright slow you down, make it work for you. Channel the extra energy you have to get your body involved in what you're saying.

- Repeat your purpose at the conclusion of your speech. If possible, tie in a related story or quote to make your words personal and easy to remember.

- The only way to be truly ready to give a speech is to practice it many times.

3

COMMUNICATING EFFECTIVELY

"**G**ood morning, Lisa," the interviewer said, extending his hand and smiling. Lisa rose as the interviewer, the company's human resources manager, came toward her. She shook his hand, but was afraid to look him directly in the eyes, so she turned her head away.

"Let's talk about your resume," the interviewer said. She followed him into his office and slumped into an upholstered chair in front of his desk. Lisa wondered what questions he might ask and whether she might be able to answer them.

"Well, what brings you to our company?" he began. "I mean, why do you want to work for us?"

"I saw your ad in the newspaper," Lisa said. "I've just graduated, and your job looked like it might be interesting."

"Hmm," the interviewer replied. Lisa could tell her answer didn't really satisfy him. But what else did he expect her to say?

✔ TRUE OR FALSE?

Can You Communicate Effectively?

1. Body language is another form of communication.

2. Never ask questions during a job interview. It will make you seem pushy.

3. The most important questions to ask your supervisor are "How do I do it?" and "Why does it have to be done?"

4. Strong customer service is key to a company's success.

Test yourself as you read through this chapter. The answers appear on pages 110–111.

"Do you know what kind of work we do here?" he asked her.

"You're in the manufacturing business," Lisa said, proud of herself for having the answer.

"Well, it's a little more than that," the interviewer said sharply. "We're a leading toy maker. In fact, one of the biggest and best in the country."

He described some of the toys they manufactured and Lisa tried to appear interested. But she kept looking down at her hands and nervously twisting the ring on her little finger. The interviewer asked several other questions and Lisa tried hard to answer them. Unfortunately, she lacked confidence in herself and never seemed to find the right words. Finally, the interviewer said to her: "The job you're applying for is in marketing. What special skills would you bring to this position?"

Lisa knew this was important. The company wasn't going to hire just anybody. "Well, I took several business courses in school," she told him. "And I'm a hard worker. As you can see on my resume, I've always had part-time jobs in school."

"Everyone who comes here works long hours," the interviewer told her. She could tell he wasn't very impressed with her answer. He glanced down at her resume again. "Do you have any other questions?"

"No, I don't think so," Lisa said. "When will I hear if I got the job?"

"We'll let you know," the interviewer told her. But as he rose and quickly escorted her to the door of his office, Lisa knew she didn't stand much of a chance of being hired.

Communication skills are important in all career modalities. As a guidance counselor, it is of the utmost importance that all avenues of communication are open and made available at all times. It is crucial for me to be able to effectively communicate with my fellow colleagues, the students and their parents, as well as the people in the community. Strong communication skills allow me to effectively relay a message to whomever I am speaking with in order to avoid any misunderstandings. Effective communication allows me to diffuse a situation; calm an angered or distraught student, parent, or teacher; and even to inspire a student to attain an educational objective. One must be able to effectively communicate with people young and old from different cultures and backgrounds. Communication skills continue to be a necessary tool for me as I attempt to make a difference in the lives of the young people who have been entrusted to me.

—Michelle Camp, guidance counselor, Azalea Gardens Middle School

JOB INTERVIEWS AND COMMUNICATION SKILLS

In the work world, communication skills are critical in many situations. These include going on job interviews, asking questions when you need help on an unfamiliar project, training other employees, and dealing with customers.

People fail to get hired because they lack effective communication skills.

Job interviews like Lisa's occur every day. People fail to get hired because they lack effective communication skills. They simply don't know how to handle an interview. "It's 90 percent chemistry," explains executive recruiter Ron Pascel. "You need to get the interviewer to like you. Good interviewees will gauge the interviewers and figure out how to fit into their organization."

How do you accomplish these goals? Some tips from career counselors and human resource managers are:

- Do your homework.
- Know your purpose.
- Watch your body language.
- Be prepared.

Do Your Homework
Whenever you write, it's essential to know your reader. And if you stand up and give a talk, you should always know your listeners. This rule also applies in a job interview. Find out as much as you can about the organization where you're interviewing. An interviewer will almost always ask if you know something about the company. "Before you even shake an interviewer's hand, find out what the company does," advises Alicia Montecalvo in *Career World* magazine. "Talk to friends or visit the library's reference section. Be sure the interviewer knows you've done your homework."

The Internet is also an excellent place to conduct research about companies. Use it to learn about a company's products and services, its employees, and countless other details that you can use during interviews.

Know Your Purpose
You go to a job interview to persuade a company to hire you. But you can accomplish this task only by

SURF THE WEB: BODY LANGUAGE

Answers.com: Body Language
http://www.answers.com/topic/body-language

Gestures: Body Language and Nonverbal
Communication
http://www.csupomona.edu/~tassi/gestures.
htm#gestures

What the Boss' Body Language Says
http://hotjobs.yahoo.com/career-articles-what_
the_boss_body_language_says-306

impressing interviewers with what you can do for their organizations. In short, take the "you" approach. In other words, ask yourself, "What can *I*, as the interviewee, do for *you*, the employer?" Your purpose is to sell the employer on you. It's not enough to simply tell an employer you'll work hard, as Lisa did. Everyone is expected to do that—you have to do more.

"Know the job and the company," advises career counselor Rozeanne Burt. "Then match what you found out to your skills."

If it's a marketing job for a toy company, explain how the courses you took in school taught you about selling to the consumer market. "You should also show your competencies in more than one sphere," Burt says. For example, your high grades in business courses may be one indication of your abilities. But you might also point out that you did volunteer work for a homeless shelter and helped them raise money. This also shows your marketing skills.

Watch Your Body Language

"Some interviewees look uninterested and don't pay attention when I talk," explains human resources director Debbie Berggren. "They look around my office. Consistent eye contact is important." Communication is not only verbal. It also involves body language. If you don't look at an interviewer

It is important to learn how to shake hands effectively. Good eye contact and a firm, but not too strong, grip are the main components of a good handshake. (Ute Kaiser, zefa/Corbis)

DRESS FOR SUCCESS: WHAT TO WEAR TO A JOB INTERVIEW

On the job interview, you need to show the interviewer that you maintain a professional demeanor. This means dressing appropriately so that your appearance works for you, rather than distracts the interviewer.

- *Don't be too casual.* Always wear a business suit. Black, navy, or dark gray are usually recommended. Women's skirts should be no shorter than knee length.

- *Be neat and clean.* Make sure that your suit is clean and wrinkle-free.

- *Be conservative.* Women should wear closed-toe shoes and nylons with a skirt. All interviewees should leave tight-fitting or revealing clothes at home.

- *Be well groomed.* Be clean-shaven and have neat hair. Avoid drastic or wild hairstyles. Don't wear excess makeup or multiple rings or earrings. Other facial piercings are probably not a good idea.

when he or she shakes your hand, you make a very poor first impression. Eye contact is also necessary during the interview. Looking at your hands, twisting your ring, or looking out the window communicates a lack of interest in the interviewer and the job.

According to JobsontheWeb.com (http://www.jobsontheweb.com), image consultants stress that you should strive for a classy, business-like

Communication is not only verbal. It also involves body language.

READING BODY LANGUAGE IN THE U.S. WORKPLACE

Poor eye contact suggests the individual has something to hide or is not confident of his or her abilities.

Crossed or folded arms suggests the person is close-minded, shy, or unapproachable.

Hands on hips conveys defensiveness.

Slouching suggests lack of focus or inattention to detail.

Busy hands conveys nervousness or unease.

Hands covering the mouth suggests the person is uneasy or has something to hide.

Weak handshake suggests a lack of confidence.

SURF THE WEB: JOB INTERVIEWS

About.com: Job Searching: Acing the Interview
http://jobsearch.about.com/cs/interviews/a/
aceinterview.htm

CareerOneStop: Resumes and Interviews
http://www.jobbankinfo.org

JobWeb: Resumes & Interviews
http://www.jobweb.com/resumes_interviews.aspx

Yahoo!hotjobs: Interviewing
http://hotjobs.yahoo.com/interview

appearance at a job interview. Your body posture is an important part of this. If you recall, Lisa slouched in the chair during her interview. This suggested that she was not sharp and alert. Experts recommend that you sit up straight and lean slightly forward. This posture shows interviewers that you're listening closely to their questions and are ready to answer them.

Be Prepared

"You can't overprepare for an interview," explains Ron Pascel. His firm carefully goes over the questions job seekers are likely to be asked and helps prospective employees develop effective answers. "You want to be in control of the interview," he says. "You want to be in the driver's seat." It often helps to rehearse the interview, just as you'd rehearse a talk in front of an audience.

Have a friend play the role of the interviewer and ask the types of questions posed to Lisa. For example, when the interviewer wants to know whether you have any questions about the job or the company, be prepared to say more than Lisa did. Ask about the types of projects you'll likely receive on the job or the growth potential and the opportunity to assume greater responsibilities. This shows that you've thought about the position and your own career goals.

By following these tips, you can usually improve your interviewing skills. You'll go into an interview feeling more confident and you'll communicate this confidence to the interviewer. This will make it more likely that you will be offered a job.

PREPARE THROUGH PRACTICE

In order to communicate effectively in an interview, you may find it helpful to conduct a few mock interviews first. Have a friend or family member ask you the following questions before you go into a real interview:

- What would you say are your top three professional strengths and weaknesses?

- What type of work environment do you prefer: quiet and private or loud and team oriented?

- How would you describe your ideal job?

HOW TO TACKLE QUESTIONS FROM LEFT FIELD

Interview questions typically focus on your background, strengths and weaknesses, and expectations for the job. But sometimes hiring managers ask questions that seem completely out of left field. OfficeTeam, a leading staffing service, asked workers to name some of the weirdest questions they've ever been asked. Some of their responses include the following:

- "Why are manhole covers round?"

- "Do you have air conditioning at home?"

- "What would I find in your refrigerator?"

- "How will taking this job change your life?"

- "What made you move to a backward city like this one?"

If the hiring manager is not crazy, he or she may actually have a goal. "Asking a truly unexpected question will likely elicit a candid, unrehearsed response," says Liz Hughes, vice president of OfficeTeam. "As a bonus, the hiring manager will get a

- What special skills would you bring to this position and this company?

- What are your expectations of this position? Of your manager?

---

better sense of the person's sense of humor and ability to think quickly."

How do you prepare for and address these types of questions? OfficeTeam provides the following advice:

- *Do some research ahead of time.* Ask your friends and family if they've ever been asked strange interview questions during an interview, how they responded to them, and what they would do differently if they received a second chance to answer the question.

- *Stay calm.* Weird questions may be off-putting, but it is important to keep your cool no matter how odd the question. Look at an offbeat question as a chance to think on your feet and provide a creative answer.

- *Have a sense of humor.* A question such as "What would I find in your refrigerator?" might be simply an icebreaker to add a little levity to a potentially stressful situation. Show that you have a sense of humor by playing the hiring manager's game and answering the question.

- What are some things you would like to avoid in a job? In a company?

- Can you describe a challenging work experience you have faced? How did you deal with it?

- What do you know about our company?

- Why did you leave your last employer?

Analyze your responses, and have your friend or family member analyze them as well. Some interviewers might even ask you what the last book you read was and how it affected you, so be ready for anything. Preparation should help you relax and communicate clearly when it is time for the real interview.

☛ FACT

Job-interview.net (http://www.job-interview.net/Bank/JobInterviewQuestions.htm) lists more than 900 sample interview questions.

PREPARE QUESTIONS OF YOUR OWN

It is a good idea to have some questions prepared when you go into an interview. This lets the interviewer know that you are interested and actively pursuing the position. In addition, this gives you a chance to make an impression on an employer—

employers like candidates who are talkative, outgoing, and curious. Here are a few suggestions:

- What is the work environment like here?
- What will my primary and secondary duties be?
- What sort of advancement potential will I have at this company?
- What information can you provide me with in regard to the stability of this company?
- What are the important skills for workers in this position?
- How frequently are performance reviews scheduled? How will my job performance be measured?
- Do you offer management training or mentorship programs for young workers?

ASK QUESTIONS ON THE JOB

David was hired by a health care company to work in their customer service department. He enjoyed talking to people, giving them information, and even handling their complaints. As part of his job, David was also expected to publish a quarterly customer newsletter. This meant that he had to understand desktop publishing. While he had seen some materials produced with desktop publishing in

(continues on page 98)

DOS AND DON'TS OF JOB INTERVIEWS

Do

- Bring several copies of your resume.

- Speak clearly; the interviewer will not be impressed if you mumble your words.

- Show your enthusiasm for the job, but don't beg for it.

- Sit up straight and maintain eye contact with the interviewer.

Don't

- Respond to the interviewer's questions with a blank stare; be prepared with good answers.

- Slouch or drape yourself over the chair—poor posture suggests to an interviewer that you are not sharp and alert. Avoiding eye contact, especially during your responses, will convey a lack of confidence.

- Bring any of your friends for moral support.

- Give the interviewer a limp-wristed handshake; it may indicate that you don't take the interview seriously.

- Use your cell phone during the interview.

- Chew gum or eat food.

✍ EXERCISE

The best way to learn more about job interviewing is to talk to people who know about it.

- Ask friends who are currently working about the types of questions they were asked in their interviews and how they answered them.

- Talk to local employers and find out what questions they ask in job interviews and the answers they expect to receive from potential employees.

- Ask a career adviser or a guidance counselor what to expect at job interviews. Write down the advice you are given and look it over before each interview.

- Speak with professors and other faculty about their experiences with job interviews. They have all been through job interviews and will likely have plenty of advice for you.

- Talk to a professional employed in your field of interest. He or she should be able to provide you with insight about how job interviews are generally carried out in this career field.

(continued from page 95)

school, David hadn't actually produced any himself. He thought when the time came for him to produce desktop publishing, he'd figure it out. As employees submitted their articles for the newsletter, David let them sit in a pile on his desk. The deadline for the first newsletter came and went, and David's manager kept asking him when it was going to be published.

"I'll have it for you soon," David promised. But when he tried using the desktop publishing system, he couldn't figure it out. He even bought a book that explained desktop publishing in simple language. It was no use; he simply did not understand the instructions.

David was in a panic. If he asked someone for help, his boss might find out. But if he didn't produce the newsletter, his boss might get angry and perhaps even fire him. What should he do?

When you are a new employee, the ability to ask the right questions may be the most important communication skill you can possess. "Don't be afraid or too proud to ask for help," explains Bradley Richardson, author of *Jobsmarts for Twentysomethings*. "How dumb will you look when you had the resources all around you, but dropped the ball because you were too afraid of looking stupid?" Richardson adds.

When you just start a job or are asked to take on an unfamiliar assignment, no one expects you to know everything. Yet many employees are timid about asking questions. Others who might have performed very well at school may feel that they know everything. They don't think they need to ask for help.

One of the keys to success on the job is asking the following questions:

- How do I do it?
- When does it have to be done?
- Why does it have to be done?

How Do I Do It?
This is the most important question to ask, but it's often far less simple than it sounds.

Suppose you're trying to put out a newsletter using desktop publishing, as David was assigned to do. Don't panic. Instead, you might start by doing some background reading to determine what you understand about the process and what you don't. Perhaps there are some new terms that seem unclear to you. The steps you need to follow in developing graphics and laying out pages may also seem mystifying. Figuring out what you don't know and making a list of questions for yourself is the best way to start coming up with the information you need. Then find someone to provide you with answers. It may be a coworker in your own department. If not, perhaps one of your coworkers can suggest someone else in another part of the organization. Make an appointment to talk to that individual; then show up with all your questions.

Don't be afraid or too proud to ask for help.

CAREERS FOR EXCELLENT COMMUNICATORS

Do you have good communications skills, but don't know what careers require this important skill? If so, you should visit the Skills Search section of O*NET Online, a U.S. government resource for occupational information. By selecting at least one of 10 basic skills, complex problem solving skills, four resource management skills, six social skills, three system skills, and 11 technical skills, you can find careers that are a good match for your abilities. Some in-demand careers that require good speaking and writing skills include:

- Chief executives
- Computer support specialists
- Counselors
- Customer service representatives
- Employment interviewers
- Engineers
- First-line supervisors/managers of food preparation and serving workers
- Flight attendants
- General and operations managers
- Insurance adjusters, examiners, and investigators
- Insurance sales agents
- Lawyers
- Medical and clinical laboratory technicians
- Medical secretaries
- Personnel recruiters
- Pharmacy technicians
- Psychologists
- Public relations specialists and managers
- Real estate sales agents
- Sales workers
- Secretaries
- Teachers
- Tour guides

In fact, hundreds of careers are listed, with information on job responsibilities and other necessary skills provided for each job. Visit http://online.onetcenter. org to use this useful career exploration tool.

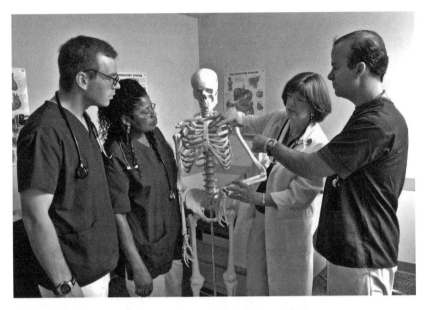

A nursing instructor teaches students about the parts of the human skeleton. The U.S. Department of Labor has identified the career of college professor as a fast-growing job that requires good communication skills. (Marty Heitner, The Image Works)

If, at first, the answer to one of your questions doesn't seem clear, ask for further explanation. One of the best approaches for finding out information is demonstrated nightly by Jim Lehrer on the PBS *NewsHour*. Lehrer insists that every guest he interviews put their answers in plain language that any viewer can understand. He is also not afraid to appear uninformed if he doesn't quite understand what the guest means. Lehrer asks the guest to make the statement in a simple manner. This is the same approach you should use when asking for information.

When Does It Have to Be Done?

You should always ask your supervisor about the deadline for completing a project. But there are other questions you might ask as well. Some projects have a fixed deadline, but others are more flexible. For example, a presentation for the national sales meeting has to be ready by the day of the meeting. For other projects, however, your supervisor might be willing to extend the deadline if necessary. Verify the project deadline with your supervisor at the beginning of the project. Also, give your supervisor frequent updates on your progress, as he or she can adjust the deadline or bring on more help if necessary.

You might also ask if there are "milestones" in the completion of the project. Does your supervisor expect to see a rough draft of the newsletter by a specific date so he can give you his comments? These milestones will help you plan a project more carefully so it will always be done by the deadline.

Why Does It Have to Be Done?

"Don't just learn how to do something," advises author Bradley Richardson, "learn why you do something!" Why is a newsletter important to the customers? How does your newsletter help other parts of the organization, such as the sales department? Learning the "whys" enables you to understand the importance of a project and strengthens your commitment to it.

ASKING GOOD QUESTIONS: STEP BY STEP

1. Figure out in advance what you don't know and what you need to know.

2. Find out from a friend or coworker who is most likely to have the answers you need.

3. Make an appointment to see that person, especially if he or she is a busy supervisor.

4. State each question as clearly and simply as possible.

5. Don't become flustered if the individual asks for clarification—put your question in different words and ask it again.

6. If at first you don't understand the answer, don't be afraid to ask for more information.

7. Thank the individual for taking time to answer your questions.

ONE TO ONE: HELPING OTHER EMPLOYEES

After you've gained some experience on a job, you may be the one assigned to train new employees. Charlene Richards works after school as an aide at a nature center. "Whenever I'm training new employees," she says, "I don't assume anything. Maybe they know a great deal; maybe they know nothing. First, I find out if they've ever had any experience doing this kind of work. If they have, then I figure they already understand something about how to care for animals. If they haven't, then I show them everything, every little detail."

Charlene tries to understand her listeners. She puts herself in their place and asks, "What would they want to know?" She can also remember her first days on the job, how nervous she was at learning everything, and how important it was to have someone explain things to her carefully.

"I know I asked a lot of dumb questions," she recalls. Fortunately, her supervisor was very patient and answered each one of them. When you are a new employee, people will expect you to ask questions, so don't hold back.

✍ EXERCISE

Select a part-time job or after-school activity. Outline your explanation of how to do the job or activity to someone who knows nothing about it. Emphasize the main points necessary to do it successfully. Deliver an oral presentation based on the outline. Ask your parents or a close friend to listen and give you feedback on it.

Charlene has prepared her training program thoroughly. There are a few key points that she repeats again and again throughout the presentation. One of these is to always follow the feeding directions on each animal's cage. She begins with an example to make her point. Charlene shows the trainees the two ferrets that currently live in the nature center and explains why they need different types of food. Cleaning the cages regularly is also important. Finally, volunteers should be alert to any signs of unusual behavior by the animals.

During the program, Charlene communicates an attitude of openness through her body language. She smiles frequently and maintains eye contact. After the program, Charlene regards herself as a resource for the volunteers. She wants to be someone they can turn to for advice while they're doing their jobs.

"It's only common sense," she says. "If you want people to do a good job, you have to give them as much support as possible. And that takes good communication." Careful preparation, a clear purpose, an understanding of your listeners, and effective use of body language—these are key elements of successful communication.

COMMUNICATING WITH CUSTOMERS

Effective communication is important not only with other people inside your organization but with people from the outside as well. No matter what

Effective communication is important not only with other people inside your organization, but with people from the outside as well.

job you hold—manufacturing or marketing, finance or public relations—you may come in contact with customers. And the impression you make tells them a great deal about your organization.

"My first impression of a company is the receptionist," says career counselor John Jarvis. He explains that he often calls a company to obtain information on its products and services to help his students who might want to apply for positions there. "If the receptionist can't explain what the company does, she will always remain a receptionist. But someone who puts the company in a good light will go on and get promotions to more responsible positions."

This is exactly what happened to Barbara. She started as a receptionist, answering the phone at a small insurance company.

"Customers would call with a problem," she said. "I'd try to put myself in their place and be as pleasant as possible, even though some of them were not always very nice. But I knew they needed to talk with one of our insurance representatives, so I'd route them to the right person as quickly as I could."

Eventually Barbara completed college and took on more responsibilities. She administered the company's benefits program and wrote its annual report. She was promoted to human resources manager. Today she interviews people seeking employment and conducts orientation programs for new employees. The orientation program enables new hires to learn about the company's benefits and other policies. Barbara also supervises a staff of three people.

"Communication," she says, "has always been a major part of my job."

Barbara worked her way up through the organization because she knew how to deal with customers in her first position as a receptionist. She realized that no company can stay in business unless it knows how to satisfy its customers and treat them properly.

✍ EXERCISE

Companies expect their workers to provide excellent customer service. With global competition increasing, customer service is the single best way—other than improving the quality of their products or services—for companies to stand out in the marketplace. How are your customer service skills? Take the following quiz to find out.

1. You are a stock clerk in a drugstore and a customer asks you where the aspirin is located. Would you:

A. Shrug your shoulders and say, "Sorry, I don't know."

B. Point in the general direction where the aspirin is located and mumble, "Over there."

C. Stop what you're doing and lead the customer to the exact spot where the aspirin products are located.

(continues)

(continued)

2. You work as a waiter in a restaurant and a customer is unhappy with his chicken pot pie. Would you:

A. Refuse to replace the food.

B. Apologize profusely and offer to replace the dish or provide a refund.

C. Call your manager and wash your hands of the problem.

3. You work as a printing sales representative and you notice that a customer missed a spelling error on a document proof. Would you:

A. Call your contact at the company to tell them about the error.

B. Show it to your coworkers and get a good laugh.

C. Let it go, figuring that if they wanted to correct the error, they would have.

Correct Answer Key: 1. C ; 2. B; 3. A

If you answered all three questions correctly, you're a master of customer service. If you answered two questions right, your customer service skills could still be improved. Remember to always make the extra effort to satisfy the needs of your customer. It will help both you and your company to be successful. If you missed all three questions, you better start from scratch and learn as much as you can about appropriate customer service. Try reading the following books to bone up on your skills: *Delivering Legendary Customer Service: Seven Steps to Success* and the *Complete Idiot's Guide to Great Customer Service.*

The general manager of a hotel once explained that customers get their first impression of his organization when they telephone for reservations. "If the person on the other end of the telephone isn't courteous," he said, "the customer immediately thinks badly of our entire hotel."

The same thing might be said for many types of service jobs. The teller at a bank, the person standing behind the counter in a fast food restaurant, the cashier at a supermarket, the online customer service representative—all of them leave a lasting impression on customers. Indeed, they are often the only people who communicate directly with customers.

If you hold one of these positions, you're responsible for what the customer thinks of the company where you work. You also have an impact on whether the customer will return to your company to do business. Remember, you make an impression on customers with not only your words: Body language is also important. A ready smile, direct eye contact, and a firm handshake are communication skills that will win you high marks whenever you deal with customers.

Whether you're interviewing for a job, learning the ropes in a new position, training other employees, or speaking with customers, you need to be a good communicator. Developing confidence in your abilities as an oral communicator takes practice. If you don't prepare for a job interview, for example, you probably won't get hired. Asking the right questions is another essential skill, even if it

A ready smile, direct eye contact, and a firm handshake are communication skills that will win you high marks whenever you deal with customers.

means exposing your ignorance. It isn't easy, but it's often what you must do to be successful on a job.

✔ TRUE OR FALSE: ANSWERS

Can You Communicate Effectively?

1. Body language is another form of communication.

True. People sometimes overlook this vital form of communication, which has the potential to convey both positive and negative signals. For example, slouching may make you seem lazy or unfocused, while standing up straight sends a message that you are confident and motivated.

2. Never ask questions during a job interview. It will make you seem pushy.

False. Asking questions during an interview will tell the hiring manager that you are interested and actively pursuing the position.

3. The most important questions to ask your supervisor are "How do I do it?" and "Why does it have to be done?"

Partially true. "How do I do it?" and "Why does it have to be done?" are key questions. But don't forget to ask "When does it have to be done?," too. Always ask your supervisor to detail when he or she wants the project completed. That way, you'll be able to organize a project into careful stages with various milestones.

4. Strong customer service is key to a company's success.

True. The quality of customer service can make or break a company. Just think of the last time you experienced poor customer service. Did you return to the establishment? Probably not. Providing excellent customer service will help your company be successful—and also get you noticed by your boss.

IN SUMMARY . . .

- Communication skills are important in many business situations, especially when interviewing for jobs, dealing with customers, training employees, and asking questions when you need help.

- The key elements of successful communication are careful preparation, a clear purpose, an understanding of your listeners, and effective use of body language.

- In order to ace an interview, do your homework first. Find out what the company is like beforehand, because employers will almost always ask what you already know about the company.

- Take the "you approach" when you go into an interview. Ask yourself: What can I do for you, the employer.

- Be aware of your body language in an interview—eye contact and posture can be just as important as what you say.

- Always prepare for job interviews. Conduct mock interviews at home and write down questions that you plan to ask the interviewer.

- There are three key questions that you should never be afraid to ask at work:
    1. How do I do it?
    2. When does it have to be done?
    3. Why does it have to be done?

4

GOOD COMMUNICATORS ARE GOOD LISTENERS

Jeff was a brilliant student. He graduated from college with a 3.8 GPA and a degree in engineering. After graduation, he received job offers from a variety of prestigious companies. He decided to work for a well-known manufacturing firm in the Midwest.

Jeff was immediately assigned to one of the teams that developed new products. The team was made up of engineers and designers as well as people from manufacturing, sales, and marketing. Jeff would have a unique opportunity to work in one of the most diverse areas of the company, and he would learn product development from the firm's most experienced team.

Unfortunately, Jeff was not much of a team player. In college, he liked working on his own and taking

✔ TRUE OR FALSE?

Are You a Good Listener?

1. It's okay to interrupt during a meeting if I have a really good point.

2. A speaker who is dressed poorly probably doesn't have anything useful to convey.

3. Good listeners have the ability to empathize with a speaker.

4. A good way to stay focused during a long presentation is to take notes.

Test yourself as you read through this chapter. The answers appear on pages 128–129.

all the credit for whatever he accomplished. Jeff soon found out that this doesn't work on teams. At meetings, he was expected to cooperate with his coworkers and listen to what they had to say. Jeff found this difficult.

"I think we may need to consider some changes in the design of this product," said one of the manufacturing supervisors at a recent team meeting. "I'm not sure . . ."

"What do you mean?" Jeff interrupted. "I think this design will work just fine." The other members of the team were stunned. How could a young engineer with almost no experience be so arrogant?

"There he goes again," one of the salespeople whispered. "He's never going to last at this company. He just won't listen to anyone."

Teamwork is the ability to work together toward a common vision. The ability to direct individual accomplishments toward organizational objectives. It is the fuel that allows common people to attain uncommon results.

**—Andrew Carnegie,
industrialist and philanthropist**

Industrialist Andrew Carnegie defined teamwork as the ability to direct personal achievements toward the goals of one's organization or company. (AP Photo)

THE ROLE OF TEAMWORK IN AN ORGANIZATION

Today, teams do much of the work inside organizations. Teams may operate inside a single area of a company, such as sales or finance. They may also comprise several different areas or functions.

People who run organizations realize that to create and sell a new product, they need input from employees with many types of expertise. In the past, these individuals might have worked on their own in different parts of the company. Now they are all brought together on teams. These *cross-functional teams*, as they are called, may not only conceptualize a new product; they may figure out how to manufacture it and how to market it to customers as well. Cross-functional teams can develop products quicker and cheaper than the more segmented offices of the past could.

THE FIVE RULES FOR EFFECTIVE LISTENING

For a team to work smoothly, its members must be able to communicate effectively. They must speak clearly and concisely so everyone understands what they are saying. They must also be willing to listen and learn from each other—this is the point of meetings. If workers are not cooperating as a team, nothing can be accomplished. Here are five rules to follow when meeting as a team:

SURF THE WEB: WORKING IN TEAMS

EffectiveMeetings.com: Team Tips
http://www.effectivemeetings.com/
teams/teamwork/teamtips.asp

Manual for Working in Teams
http://www.analytictech.com/mb021/
teamhint.htm

Surviving the Group Project: A Note on
Working in Teams
http://web.cba.neu.edu/~ewertheim/
teams/ovrvw2.htm#Introduction

Team Building
http://www.meetingwizard.org/
meetings/team-building.cfm

13 Ways to Encourage Teamwork
http://www.askmen.com/money/
successful_100/115_success.html

1. Don't interrupt.

2. Don't jump to conclusions.

3. Don't judge the messenger.

4. Don't be self-centered.

5. Don't tune out.

Don't Interrupt

Teams can't function efficiently if resentment has built up among different members.

How many times has someone interrupted what you're trying to say? Perhaps it was one of your parents, a friend, or even a coworker. Chances are you felt pretty irritated. Some people don't mean to be rude. They just can't seem to control themselves. They are so eager to express their opinion that they simply can't wait for the speaker to finish.

Unfortunately, teams don't operate well when others interrupt. Everyone deserves an equal chance to be heard. If an employee is cut off in mid-sentence, is interrupted while presenting an important idea, he or she is likely to feel unappreciated. This worker may even begin to feel resentful. Teams can't function efficiently if resentment has built up among different members. Imagine trying to run a basketball team on which the players don't get along with each other. The spirit of teamwork disappears, and the team might even have less desire to win.

Interrupting might also prevent an employee from saying something vital to the future of the team and the success of its project. In the best teams, every team member has a chance to contribute.

Don't Jump to Conclusions

Allison worked at Fairway Cleaners for a few hours each week after school and on Saturdays. When customers came in, she took their cleaning and wrote up a ticket describing the customers' requested service. The ticket had to include every item that belonged

NOSTUESO

City Year, a Boston-based, nationwide nonprofit service organization, has an interesting policy for all its meetings: Most use a ground rule called NOSTUESO to keep wordy employees from monopolizing discussions and to ensure that all voices are heard. NOSTUESO is an acronym that stands for "No One Speaks Twice Until Everybody Speaks Once."

Source: *Inc.* (http://www.inc.com)

to the customer and indicate the exact day when the customer wanted to have his or her cleaning ready to pick up. Accuracy was important.

One day while Allison was working, Mrs. Carlson entered the store. Mrs. Carlson was one of Fairway's most loyal customers. She usually left her cleaning on Saturday and wanted it a week later.

"Good morning, Mrs. Carlson," Allison said with a smile. "That's a big load of cleaning this week."

"We just got back from summer vacation," Mrs. Carlson said. "Our family goes through a lot of clothing. My husband has a business trip next Thursday so I'll be in on Wednesday to pick all this up." She put the pants in one pile, shirts in another,

Strong listening skills are especially important in service industry careers. (Charles Rex Arbogast, AP Photo)

and sweaters in a third. "I think there are five pairs of pants," Mrs. Carlson began.

But Allison was already moving ahead of her. She was counting the items of clothes herself and putting all the necessary information on Mrs. Carlson's ticket. Allison indicated that the cleaning would be ready in a week—the way Mrs. Carlson usually wanted it.

"Have a nice weekend," Allison said, as she handed over the ticket.

"Thanks, Allison," Mrs. Carlson said. "I'll see you in a few days."

"That's funny," Allison thought. "It'll be a whole week before I see her again.

Late Wednesday afternoon, Allison came into the cleaners after her last class. Mrs. Carlson was there, talking to Allison's boss. "There's been a terrible mistake," her boss said angrily. "Mrs. Carlson specifically told you that this cleaning was supposed to be ready on Wednesday. Now she's stopped in on her way home from work and it isn't here. Her husband's leaving on a business trip tomorrow and he needs these clothes."

Allison didn't know what to say. "I . . . I just assumed, Mrs. Carlson, that you always want your cleaning on Saturday."

Allison's boss was very upset. "Customers have varying needs, Allison. You had better start listening if you want to keep working here."

☛ FACT

The average speaker talks at about 160 words per minute, but we can absorb information at three times that rate. However, according to one study, we listen with only 25 percent efficiency. This accounts for many of the misunderstandings that occur on the job.

Good listening skills will make you a better employee.

Since we can process information much faster than someone speaks, it's easy to stop paying attention to the speaker and begin thinking about something else. That's exactly what happened to Allison. She assumed she knew what Mrs. Carlson wanted and jumped to the wrong conclusion.

Whenever you receive instructions on a job, it's important to listen carefully. Don't assume you know what the speaker is going to say. If a customer is asking you to do something, listen to everything he or she has to say. If your boss is speaking, listen carefully and don't jump to the wrong conclusion. Good listening skills will make you a better employee.

Don't Judge the Messenger

Sometimes we let our opinions of a speaker prevent us from listening carefully to what is being said. One manager from the Northeast explained that she was used to dealing with people who speak quickly and that she likes to talk pretty fast herself. She admitted that whenever she has to listen to someone who talks slowly, she begins to get impatient and even stops listening. "Why can't they just get to the point?" she said.

Whether we like to admit it or not, each of us has certain biases, which may get in the way of effective listening. Some common biases are triggered by the following questions:

- *How does the speaker sound?* If a person
  has an unfamiliar accent, you may find
  yourself judging what he or she is going to
  say without really listening. Perhaps this
  individual comes from a different region of
  the country or a different part of the world.
  Perhaps he or she speaks more quickly
  or more slowly than you. None of these
  reasons excuse jumping to conclusions and
  dismissing what the speaker may say before
  first giving him or her a fair chance.

- *What does the speaker look like?* The first
  thing you notice about people is their
  appearance. What kind of clothes do they
  have? How much jewelry do they wear?
  It's easy to let someone's appearance—
  especially someone who looks different
  from you—stand in the way of effective
  communication. In his book *Are You
  Communicating? You Can't Manage Without
  It*, Donald Walton points out that judging
  people based on appearance is one of the
  emotional obstacles that can prevent you
  from giving rational consideration to what
  someone is saying.

  For example, suppose the supermarket
  where you work hires a new cashier who
  is assigned the checkout counter next to
  yours. He's done this kind of work before
  and offers you some suggestions that

Age can be an enormous barrier to effective communication.

might make your job easier. But you think he looks odd, so you don't listen. Walton urges that people concentrate on what the speaker is saying rather than who is saying it. Ask, is it true? Does it sound right to me? Is it contrary to or in line with the facts that I've previously heard? Walton says that these are the questions you should consider instead of focusing on appearances.

* *How old is the speaker?* Age can be an enormous barrier to effective communication. If a person has gray hair, you may assume that he or she can't relate to you. Likewise, some adults feel that a teenager is too young or inexperienced to teach them anything. This is another example of an emotional generalization that can prevent effective listening. Instead, individuals and their messages should be evaluated on their own merits.

Put Yourself in the Speaker's Place

Corey works as an assistant at a large veterinary hospital. Clients bring in their pets not only for routine visits, but for serious illnesses and major operations. Corey assists the veterinarian with many kinds of services to the animals.

"It's important to understand why the animal is there and what the owner is feeling," Corey explains. "If the client is worried, I pick up on that.

I listen to what they say and watch their body language. Then I try to make small talk to help them feel better."

Sometimes a client will call the hospital after a pet has undergone surgery to find out how the animal is doing. "If the doctor is busy," Corey explains, "I may take the call and talk to the customers. I know they're worried and I try to understand that. I give them all the information I can. I tell them how their animal is feeling, whether the anesthesia has worn off—anything that will reassure owners that their pet is all right."

Good listeners have the ability to empathize with a speaker.

Good listeners have the ability to empathize with a speaker. They try to read the speaker's body language. Perhaps the speaker has a pained expression or looks tense. Any of these clues may indicate that he or she is nervous. A halting style of speech or emotional tone of voice may also indicate that the individual is upset.

Listeners can then use what management consultant Ron Meis calls "openers" and "encouragers" to enable the speaker to communicate more easily. The listener might say, "It looks to me that there's something you'd like to talk about," or "Is something bothering you?" These openers may get the speaker started. Listeners can also communicate their interest in what the speaker is saying by nodding their heads, making eye contact with the speaker, or using phrases such as "that's interesting." These signals encourage the speaker to keep talking.

☞ FACT

How do we communicate a message? Only 7 percent of our message comes through the words we use, 38 percent comes through our tone of voice, and 55 percent comes through our body language.

Don't Tune Out: Find Something of Interest

In school, we are required to sit through many hours of classes. On the job, we will be required to sit through many meetings and training sessions. If we allow ourselves to get bored and start daydreaming, chances are we won't listen very carefully to what's being said. How do you beat boredom?

One way is to look for something of value in what the speaker is saying—something that can benefit you. For example, suppose you've just gone to work at a new company, and you're sitting through a two-day orientation program. At this orientation, speakers from various departments talk about their operations and how they contribute to the company's success. These programs can be long and tedious—if you approach them that way. Or they can give you a chance to find out where you might eventually like to work in the organization. Perhaps one department sounds particularly interesting, with plenty of opportunity for growth. This might be the place for you to set your sights.

✍ EXERCISE

Are you a good listener? If you can identify with these statements, you have effective listening skills.

- I usually allow a speaker to finish talking without interrupting.
- I don't jump to conclusions when someone is talking but listen carefully.
- I don't evaluate a speaker by the way he or she looks or sounds. I listen to the message.
- I try to put myself in the speaker's shoes and treat him or her the way I would want to be treated.
- I concentrate on the speaker and don't let distractions get in the way.
- If I disagree with someone, I hold my comments until he or she stops talking.
- When I'm listening, I listen to the speaker's tone of voice and take note of his or her body language.
- When someone speaks, I usually try to look for something valuable in what is said.

To stay focused during a long presentation, it also helps to take notes.

To stay focused during a long presentation, it also helps to take notes. You don't have to worry about all the details; just listen for the main ideas and write them down. This will help you to concentrate and avoid becoming distracted. Some presentations are followed by question-and-answer sessions. It's often a good idea to formulate questions while you are listening to the speaker. This is another way to concentrate on what he or she is saying, avoid boredom, and focus your attention on the main ideas. Good questions will provide you with additional information. Asking questions also gives you a way to stand out from most of your peers and show your superiors that you are listening carefully to what they're saying.

✔ TRUE OR FALSE: ANSWERS

Are You a Good Listener?

1. It's okay to interrupt during a meeting if I have a really good point.

False. Teams don't operate well when people interrupt. Always wait for the speaker to conclude his or her presentation before you offer your opinion—even if you think you have a world-class idea.

2. A speaker who is poorly dressed probably doesn't have anything useful to convey.

False. It's important to avoid giving in to subtle biases we bring to any interaction, such as those pertaining to a speaker's appearance, race, accent, or age. Focus on the quality of the information being conveyed, not the messenger.

3. Good listeners have the ability to empathize with a speaker.

True. Good listeners are careful observers of a speaker's body language, style of speech, and tone of voice. They use these cues to empathize with and understand the speaker—which encourages better communication.

4. A good way to stay focused during a long presentation is to take notes.

True. Taking notes will help keep you from falling asleep during a meeting (don't laugh, it's happened to some of the best workers). Better yet, it will tell your coworkers that you are interested in the presentation and help you formulate questions in case it is followed by a question-and-answer session.

IN SUMMARY . . .

- Group meetings and teamwork are essential parts of the working world today.
- The most effective teams allow every member to contribute during meetings.

Listening to everyone's ideas and opinions is critical.

- There are five rules to effective listening:
  1. Don't interrupt.
  2. Don't jump to conclusions.
  3. Don't judge the messenger.
  4. Don't be selfish.
  5. Don't tune out.

MAKING MEETINGS WORK

Harold leaned back in his seat and sighed wearily. The assistant sales manager had been talking steadily for almost 25 minutes and showed no signs of slowing down. "Why does he always go on so long?" Harold wondered. "He just puts all of us to sleep."

Slowly, Harold began tuning out his boss's presentation as his mind wandered to more pleasant topics. He thought about his vacation that was coming up soon. Harold had made reservations at a beautiful hotel on the beach. More important, he was planning to spend the entire week without his beeper or cell phone.

"I won't have to hear the boss's voice for seven days," Harold thought. "What could be more wonderful?"

His mind then drifted to the big sale he completed yesterday. A regular customer had more than doubled her usual order. A smile crossed Harold's

✔ TRUE OR FALSE?

Are You a Master of Meetings?

1. Every successful meeting needs an agenda.

2. Everyone in my work group should attend meetings.

3. It's okay to disagree with someone in a meeting as long as you do so respectfully.

4. The best virtual meetings are those in which the participants use the same technology.

Test yourself as you read through this chapter. The answers appear on pages 148–149.

lips. "Yes," he nodded to himself, "that was a job well done."

Suddenly, Harold's daydreaming was interrupted. "Harold," his boss said with a hearty laugh, "I want to thank you for nodding your head and volunteering to take on this important project."

Whoever invented the meeting must have had Hollywood in mind. I think they should consider giving Oscars for meetings: Best Meeting of the Year, Best Supporting Meeting, Best Meeting Based on Material from Another Meeting.

—William Goldman, American author

Harold was stunned. He turned to one of his coworkers at the meeting. "What project?" he whispered.

"Writing the big report that's due in two weeks," she said.

"But, I can't," Harold told her. "I'm going on vacation!"

"No, you're not," his boss replied. "It just got canceled."

THE IMPORTANCE OF MEETINGS

In business, meetings are a fact of life. Project teams get together for meetings. Salespeople meet customers. New employees meet for training sessions. According to consultants Roger Mosvick and Robert Nelson, authors of *We've Got to Start Meeting Like This! A Guide to Successful Meeting Management,* the number of business meetings is growing. But that doesn't mean that people are getting more work done. Indeed, Mosvick and Nelson report that "over 50 percent of the productivity of the billions of meeting hours is wasted." Why? Poor meeting preparation, they explain, and lack of training on how to conduct meetings effectively are the culprits. As a result, employees tend to tune out and fail to participate. A well-run meeting combines the writing, speaking, and listening skills that we've been discussing in this book. Whether you're leading a meeting or are just a participating in one, you need to communicate clearly.

Whether you're leading a meeting or are just a participating in one, you need to communicate clearly.

☛ FACT

Managers and organization professionals spend one-fourth of their week in meetings.

Good communication skills are vital for a healthy and successful work environment. Good communication enables an efficient workplace in which issues are quickly identified and resolved. The best form of communication for a given situation is one that fully conveys the intended message in a timely manner. Sometimes it is necessary to have face-to-face meetings or team conferences, but other times simple communication methods like email or telephone conversations are more appropriate and can be more efficient. It is important for everyone in the workplace to understand how best to use various communication skills as well as ensuring the free-flow of information.

—Thomas Ainsworth, design engineer,
Northrop Grumman

PLANNING AN AGENDA

A group of high school seniors were meeting to talk about the class prom. It was the third time that all of them had come together, and the discussion went on for two hours. It was a free-for-all, with every-

During meetings, it is important to listen closely to the ideas of your coworkers. (Ellen Senisi, The Image Works)

body expressing his or her opinions. But by the end of the meeting, there was still no agreement on what should be done for the prom.

In a large office building, a group of managers sat around discussing the annual company outing. They talked and talked. They traded stories about past company outings. Then they complained to each other about problems in their departments. Finally, they started to wonder whether there should be an outing at all this year. After three hours, nothing had been accomplished, even though all the outing arrangements were supposed to be finalized by the end of the week.

SURF THE WEB: IMPROVE YOUR MEETINGS

EffectiveMeetings.com
http://www.effectivemeetings.com

Meeting Wizard
http://www.meetingwizard.com

Mind Tools: Running Effective Meetings
http://www.mindtools.com/CommSkll/
RunningMeetings.htm

Work911.com: Effective Meetings
http://www.work911.com/articles/
meetmgt.htm

As seen in the two preceding examples, meetings can often become long-winded talkfests where nothing is ever accomplished. One way to avoid this problem is to carefully structure the meeting. That structure of a meeting is called an *agenda*. As authors Richard Chang and Kevin Kehoe explain in *Meetings That Work! A Practical Guide to Shorter and More Productive Meetings*, "Just as the developer works from a blueprint and shares it with other people working on the building, a meeting should have a 'blueprint.' . . . The blueprint for any meeting is its agenda, which provides everyone with a picture of what the meeting will look like."

The most critical element of any meeting agenda is the *objective,* which addresses the purpose of the meeting. If you're writing a memo or report, your first job is to determine its purpose and describe it in the introduction. Similarly, if you're leading a meeting, one of your responsibilities is to establish its objectives, making sure they are described in the agenda.

The most critical element of any meeting agenda is the objective, which addresses the purpose of the meeting.

When developing an agenda, write a sentence for each objective. Similar to when you are writing or speaking, short summary sentences tell the participants what you want to cover in the meeting and what you hope to accomplish. This way you can avoid a rambling meeting that goes off in the wrong direction.

For example, suppose you're in charge of planning the class prom. Your meeting's objective might be: *Generate a list of four possible places to hold the prom.* Your next step would be to set a date, time, and place for the meeting. Punctuality is important. If people are wandering in late, it only disrupts and drags out the meeting. Sometimes you even find yourself wasting more time explaining important points all over again for latecomers' benefit. Unlike in student club meetings, in business meetings your boss may be a stickler for punctuality. As one manager put it, "If they show up five minutes late, I usually tell them to forget it."

SURF THE WEB: SAMPLE MEETING AGENDAS

Check out these sites for examples of meeting agendas from national and local governments and educational institutions.

City of Tulsa, Oklahoma
http://www.cityoftulsa.org/agendas

Colorado Springs City Council & City Management
http://www.springsgov.com/agendas.asp

The Regents of the University of California
http://www.universityofcalifornia.edu/regents/meetings.html

School District of New Richmond
http://www.newrichmond.k12.wi.us/main/board/agenda.cfm

PEOPLE AND PREPARATION

In a study of executives conducted by the Wharton Center for Applied Research at the University of Pennsylvania, a majority reported that there are too many people participating at meetings. Many meetings include people who do not need to be there. Participants who do not make meaningful contributions to meetings simply burden productive attendants. When a meeting becomes unwieldy, far less is accomplished. Only invite people who absolutely have to attend.

Give participants the meeting agenda in advance if you want them to do any preparation. For example, suppose you want someone to report on the location of last year's prom. This information might influence the selection for this year's prom. Or perhaps you want participants to read an article from the school library that lists the elements of successful school proms. If participants receive the agenda in advance, they can do all the necessary preparation. This will make the meeting more productive.

When a meeting becomes unwieldy, far less is accomplished.

A report from the Annenberg School for Communication at the University of Southern California found that most meetings occur with minimal notice and no written agenda. As a result, meetings often seem ineffective. You can avoid this problem by carefully developing a set of objectives, defining the logistics of the meeting, limiting the number of participants, and insisting that everyone prepare.

Finally, your agenda should list the meeting's activities. All activities should be designed to carry out the objectives of the meeting.

For example, if you're leading the prom-planning meeting, your activities might be as follows:

1. Provide a brief introduction.

2. Report on last year's prom.

3. Discuss the article you asked everybody to read.

4. Discuss possible locations for this year's event.

5. Appoint a committee to investigate potential locations and write a summary report.

6. Set a date for the next meeting.

✍ EXERCISE

Think about the last meeting you attended for a class project or student club. Copy the sample agenda form and fill in the appropriate information based on what went on during your meeting. What was the objective of the meeting? Did all of the people who attended need to be there? Did the meeting last longer than necessary? Could it have been organized or planned better?

EFFECTIVE SPEAKING

Suppose you have to lead a meeting for your work team. You'll probably need to make a short presentation at the beginning of the meeting, welcoming participants and explaining the agenda. This requires effective speaking skills. As you begin the talk, explain your objectives clearly. And be sure you add energy to your delivery.

SAMPLE MEETING AGENDA FORM

Objectives: _____

_____

_____

_____

Date: _____ Time: _____

Location: _____

Participants: _____

_____

_____

_____

Preparation: _____

_____

_____

Activities: _____

1. _____

2. _____

3. _____

4. _____

Speaking with energy can keep people involved and prevent them from daydreaming or even falling asleep!

If you've ever heard speakers who talk in a dull monotone, you know how boring it can sound. Speaking with energy can keep people involved and prevent them from daydreaming or even falling asleep! You can add energy with your voice by emphasizing certain words or ideas as you speak to indicate their importance. By changing your speaking volume, you can also add variety to your presentation.

Gestures are another way to add energy. As you talk, use your hands to reinforce what you're saying. For example, if you're listing three objectives, use your fingers to indicate the first, second, and third points. If you're making a key point, try jabbing the air with your forefinger. Or if you're asking support from participants at the meeting, stretch out your hands to them. Gestures automatically raise the vocal energy of your talk. In fact, if you use gestures, it's almost impossible to speak in a monotone.

Nothing builds rapport faster than eye contact. Building rapport is critical for achieving audience buy-in—and without 100 percent buy-in, it's terribly difficult to inspire an audience to act.

—Tony Jeary in Inspire Any Audience: Proven Secrets of the Pros for Powerful Presentations

Making eye contact with your listeners is another way to keep them involved. As you begin a thought, look at one listener. Continue looking at that individual until you complete the thought. Then select another listener and repeat the process. This enables you to establish a dialogue with all participants, which is an effective way to keep them focused on what you're saying.

LISTENING IS CRUCIAL—EVEN IF YOU DISAGREE

As you read in Chapter 4, you can listen at a much faster rate than you speak. If you're not careful, this

✍ EXERCISE

Ask a friend to listen to you speak about the events of your day, taking note of your use of energy. Ask this friend to rate you from 1 (poor) to 5 (excellent) on the following:

- Did you speak with enthusiasm?
- Did you raise your voice level to emphasize certain words?
- Did you use gestures to reinforce your ideas?
- Did you make eye contact with your listener?
- Did you keep your listener involved?

can create problems. Suppose you work in your company's customer service department. You're sitting at a meeting where one of your colleagues is presenting her plan to serve customers more rapidly. Part of the way through her presentation, you decide that her plan won't work. But instead of listening to the rest of it, you immediately begin to write out a *rebuttal*, or opposing argument. By not listening to the rest of her plan, you may miss some key points that may persuade you that her plan will actually work. At the very least, listening may help you shape a better rebuttal. By listening to each of her main points, you might be able to challenge all, instead of a portion, of her plan.

Every rebuttal should be presented as respectfully as possible. That is, you must know how to disagree with others politely. If you think someone's idea won't work, it does no good to say it's "stupid." This type of comment simply insults your colleague. The goal of a meeting is not to demonstrate your own intelligence by "one-upping" someone else. This just creates hard feelings. The goal of each meeting is to create a good working atmosphere among the participants. By working together you should be able to increase each other's effectiveness. It's almost impossible to work together, however, if a meeting is being torn apart by serious disagreements. These must be handled very carefully.

First, find something positive to say about another employee's proposal, even if you disagree with it. By starting on a positive note, you can demonstrate at least some support for your coworker. You can also show your appreciation for the hard work he or she put into the proposal.

Find something positive to say about another employee's proposal, even if you disagree with it.

Second, don't come on too strong. Present your disagreement gently. Use phrases such as "I think," or "Maybe we should consider," or "Perhaps there's another way to look at this." You don't want to sound like a know-it-all.

Third, enlist support from other people at the meeting. After you've presented your ideas, ask them what they think. Often the leader will step in at this point and ask other people at the meeting to express their views. This may enable everyone to reach some general agreement.

People who disagree have an argument, but people who dissent have a quarrel. . . . Disagreement is the lifeblood of democracy, dissension is its cancer.

—Daniel J. Boorstin, U.S. historian

CONCLUDING A MEETING

As Richard Chang and Kevin Kehoe point out, the leader's role is to make sure the meeting follows the agenda. A meeting that stays on track is less likely to consume needless time. A leader is also responsible for reviewing any decisions and actions that are taken at a meeting. This review makes certain that everyone fully understands the decisions and actions.

Many meetings conclude with one or more plans of action. This often ensures that a meeting accomplishes a meaningful goal. For example, suppose you and your colleagues at the customer service meeting decide on two courses of action to improve service. First, you will answer customer calls after only a single ring of the telephone. Second, if you don't know the answer to a customer's question, you will get back to him or her by the next business day. You and your colleagues need to agree to carry out these steps and report the results at the next meeting.

Generally, participants try to reach a consensus on their decisions and actions. This process is easier in a meeting where the spirit of cooperation prevails. If everyone feels that he or she has been heard and that his or her opinions have been respected, an agreement is much easier to attain.

THE WORLD OF VIRTUAL MEETINGS

Virtual meetings, in which one or more participants use the Internet or the telephone (sometimes augmented by Web technology) to communicate with coworkers, are very popular in the business world today. In fact, the global market for Web conferencing services is estimated at more than $700 million annually. While web- and teleconferencing save companies money and time, they can also present challenges to participants. For example, it may be difficult to set up a meeting time that works for a company's employees in New York, Tokyo, and Berlin. Here are a few tips that will help you to successfully communicate during web meetings.

- *Pay attention.* Resist the urge to let your focus wander when not actively participating.

- *Be discriminating regarding information.* Be selective when choosing what information you convey during a virtual meeting. Save some details for subsequent emails or memos.

- *Clarify confusing conversations.* The technology for virtual meetings has improved greatly, but it is still no substitute for face-to-face meetings. If a participant says something you don't understand or a document is referred that you cannot view, speak up so you can understand what is being discussed.

- *Get everyone online.* Encourage your boss to set up web meetings in which all parties are online. This will help participants to view documents and presentations in the same format—reducing the need for momentum-breaking stops to clarify confusing issues.

✔ TRUE OR FALSE: ANSWERS

Are You a Master of Meetings?

1. Every successful meeting needs an agenda.

True. Every successful meeting features an agenda that was prepared ahead of time that details its objectives. Creating an agenda will help you and your coworkers stay focused and save time.

2. Everyone in my work group should attend meetings.

False. Workers believe that meetings are the biggest time-waster at work, according to a nationwide survey by OfficeTeam. Many believe this because they are often included in meetings in which they do not really need to attend. Meetings that only include the key members of a project will proceed faster and be more focused.

3. It's okay to disagree with someone in a meeting as long as you do so respectfully.

True. It's okay to disagree with a coworker as long as you do so in a respectful manner. If you disagree with a coworker during a meeting, wait to hear the person out (so you don't miss important points that may actually convince you that the individual is right or so that you can gather information to support your argument). Once your coworker finishes, disagree politely and professionally by first praising certain aspects of his or her idea, and then calmly stating what you would do differently. Never use insulting language when disagreeing with a coworker. Try to avoid creating a one-on-one personality clash by soliciting the opinions of your coworkers.

4. The best virtual meetings are those in which the participants use the same technology.

True. Virtual meetings are most effective when every participant is communicating in the same manner (using the same Web or teleconferencing technology) and viewing documents in an identical format.

IN SUMMARY . . .

- Without proper preparation, meetings can be a waste of time.

- Agendas are critical to keeping a meeting on track and keeping all participants informed.

- Agendas must list one or more objectives, which state the purpose of the meeting.

- Invite only the necessary people to meetings to keep the group focused and active.

- When leading a meeting, speak with energy, tone variability, and hand gestures.

- Maintain eye contact with your listeners.
- Listen carefully and completely before preparing to disagree with someone.
- At the end of the meeting, summarize all the actions or decisions that were made to be sure everyone is in agreement.

WEB SITES

Body Language

Answers.com: Body Language
http://www.answers.com/topic/body-language

Gestures: Body Language and Nonverbal
Communication
http://www.csupomona.edu/~tassi/gestures.
htm#gestures

What the Boss' Body Language Says
http://hotjobs.yahoo.com/career-articles-what_
the_boss_body_language_says-306

General

Free Management Library: Communications Skills
http://www.managementhelp.org/commskls/
cmm_face.htm

MindTools: Communication Skills
http://www.mindtools.com/page8.html

O*NET OnLine
http://online.onetcenter.org

Work911.com
http://www.work911.com

Job Search

About.com: Job Searching: Acing the Interview
http://jobsearch.about.com/cs/interviews/a/
aceinterview.htm

About.com: Job Searching: Resumes, Cover Letters,
and Employment-Related Letters
http://jobsearch.about.com/od/resumes/u/
resumesandletters.htm

Career Lab: Cover Letters
http://www.careerlab.com/letters

CareerOneStop: Resumes and Interviews
http://www.jobbankinfo.org

CollegeGrad.com: Cover Letters
http://www.collegegrad.com/coverletters

CollegeGrad.com: Resumes
http://www.collegegrad.com/resume

Job-interview.net
http://www.job-interview.net/Bank/
JobInterviewQuestions.htm

JobStar Central: About Cover Letters
http://www.jobstar.org/tools/resume/cletters.php

JobStar Central: Resumes
http://www.jobstar.org/tools/resume

JobWeb: Resumes & Interviews
http://www.jobweb.com/resumes_interviews.aspx

Monster Career Advice: Resume & Letters
http://career-advice.monster.com/resume-tips/
home.aspx

Quintessential Careers: Cover Letter Resources for
Job-Seekers
http://www.quintcareers.com/covres.html

The Riley Guide: Resumes & Cover Letters
http://www.rileyguide.com/letters.html

Vault.com: Resumes and Advice
http://www.vault.com/index.jsp

Vault.com: Sample Cover Letters
http://www.vault.com/nr/ht_list.jsp?ht_type=9

Yahoo! HotJobs: Interviewing
http://hotjobs.yahoo.com/interview

Meetings

EffectiveMeetings.com
http://www.effectivemeetings.com

GlobalKnowledge: How to Avoid Meetings—or at
Least the Unproductive Ones
http://www.findwhitepapers.com/whitepaper139

Meeting Wizard
http://www.meetingwizard.com

Mind Tools: Running Effective Meetings
http://www.mindtools.com/CommSkll/
RunningMeetings.htm

Public Speaking

The Art of Using Humor in Public
http://www.squaresail.com/auh.html

How to Use Humor in Public Speaking
http://www.expertvillage.com/video/5830_
public-speaking-humor.htm

Humor in Public Speaking
http://www.msstate.edu/org/toastmasters/
resources/humor_in_speaking.pdf

Public Speaking Expert: Using Humour in a Speech
http://www.publicspeakingexpert.co.uk/
UsingHumourInASpeech.html

WannaLearn.com: Personal Enrichment: Public
Speaking
http://www.wannalearn.com/Personal_
Enrichment/Public_Speaking

Teamwork

Manual for Working in Teams
http://www.analytictech.com/mb021/teamhint.
htm

Surviving the Group Project: A Note on Working in
Teams
http://web.cba.neu.edu/~ewertheim/teams/
ovrvw2.htm#Introduction

Team Building
http://www.meetingwizard.org/meetings/team-
building.cfm

13 Ways to Encourage Teamwork
http://www.askmen.com/money/success-ful_100/115_success.html

Writing

About.com: Writing Skills
http://careerplanning.about.com/cs/miscskills/a/writing_skills.htm

Blogger
https://www.blogger.com/start

Write It Well Blog
http://www.writeitwell.com

GLOSSARY

active voice speaking or writing in a style that puts the subject at the front of the sentence; this makes communication more concise and bold; example The manager gave a speech at the conference. (See **passive voice** for comparison.)

agenda a detailed structure for a meeting that explains what is to be covered

cover letter also called an application letter, this briefly describes your interests in a job and your qualifications

bias a prejudice that influences your actions and thoughts

blog a Web site that presents an individual's opinions or information about a particular topic or topics; most contain text, images, and links to other blogs or online resources and allow visitors to respond to the comments made by the blogger

body language the gestures, movements, and mannerisms a person uses to intentionally or unintentionally communicate moods and opinions to others

cold cover letter an unprompted cover letter that is sent to a company that has not advertised job openings; also known as an uninvited cover letter

cross-functional team a group of employees from different departments of a company brought together to solve a problem or accomplish a task as a team

describe to give an account of something or someone in words

dynamic energetic writing and speaking, using words that are active, expressive, and succinct

email electronic mail, which is sent via computer and telephone and cable lines from one person to another

explain to make something more understandable, often addressing *why* an action has occurred

4 Cs key traits of effective writing; to be successful, one's writing must be concise, compelling, clear, and correct

listener analysis an evaluation of your audience to help you prepare for a talk

milestones checkpoints during the process of completing a project intended to insure that the final deadline will be met

monotone speech that sounds one-toned, lacking in energy and variability (something to avoid when speaking in front of an audience)

objective the purpose or reason for a meeting or other event

"one-upping" competing, trying to stay ahead of or "one-up" someone else

"openers" or "encouragers" phrases that urge someone to communicate with you (example, "Is there something troubling you?")

passive voice the style of speech and writing that buries the subject in the sentence, which should be avoided; example: At the conference, the speech was given by the manager. (See **active voice** for comparison.)

persuade to encourage others to take a course of action

pyramid style an approach to writing in which the most important information is placed at the beginning

rebuttal an argument against another person's position

receiver in this book, the listener or reader

resume a brief listing of your job objective, education, and job experience that is used to apply for employment

sender in this book, the speaker or writer

stage fright fear of speaking in front of an audience

summary sentences sentences that summarize the purpose of a piece of writing

3 Ts an effective method of organizing a presentation by telling your audience about your topic in the introduction, telling them about it in the body of your speech, and telling them about it again in your conclusion

teaser the beginning of a story, speech, movie, or television program that hooks the audience and encourages them to continue to read, listen, or watch

Twitter an Internet utility that allows users to communicate their opinions, activities, and other information to friends and family; messages can only be 140 characters in length

BIBLIOGRAPHY

Andersen, Peter. *The Complete Idiot's Guide to Body Language*. New York: Alpha, 2004.

Anderson, Laura Killen. *McGraw-Hill's Proofreading Handbook*. 2d ed. New York: McGraw-Hill, 2006.

Baude, Dawn-Michelle. *The Executive Guide to Email Correspondence: Including Model Letters for Every Situation*. Franklin Lakes, N.J.: Career Press, 2006.

Beatty, Richard H. *175 High-Impact Cover Letters*. 3d ed. Hoboken, N.J.: Wiley, 2008.

Bly, Robert W., and Regina Anne Kelly. *The Encyclopedia of Business Letters, Faxes, and Emails: Features Hundreds of Model Letters, Faxes, and Emails to Give Your Business Writing the Attention It Deserves*. Rev. ed. Franklin Lakes, N.J.: Career Press, 2009.

Cappon, Rene J. *The Associated Press Guide to Punctuation*. New York: Basic Books, 2003.

Clark, Roy Peter. *Writing Tools: 50 Essential Strategies for Every Writer*. New York: Little, Brown and Company, 2008.

Covey, Stephen R. *The 7 Habits of Highly Effective People.* 15th ed. New York: The Free Press, 2004.

Covey, Sean. *The 7 Habits of Highly Effective Teens.* New York: Fireside Press, 1998.

Editors of The American Heritage Dictionaries. *100 Words Almost Everyone Confuses and Misuses.* Boston: Houghton Mifflin, 2004.

———. *100 Words Every High School Graduate Should Know.* Boston: Houghton Mifflin, 2003.

Enelow, Wendy S., and Louise Kursmark. *Cover Letter Magic: Trade Secrets of Professional Resume Writers.* 3d ed. Indianapolis, Ind.: JIST Works, 2006.

Farr, Michael. *The Quick Resume & Cover Letter Book: Write and Use an Effective Resume in Only One Day.* 4th ed. Indianapolis, Ind.: JIST Works, 2007.

Fogarty, Mignon. *Grammar Girl's Quick and Dirty Tips for Better Writing.* New York: Holt Paperbacks, 2008.

Fox, Sue. *Etiquette For Dummies.* 2d ed. Hoboken, N.J.: For Dummies, 2007.

Gallagher, Richard S. *Delivering Legendary Customer Service: Seven Steps to Success.* Bangor, Maine: Booklocker.com, 2005.

Gilad, Suzanne. *Copyediting & Proofreading For Dummies.* Hoboken, N.J.: For Dummies, 2007.

Greene, Brenda. *Get the Interview Every Time: Fortune 500 Hiring Professionals' Tips for Writing Winning*

Resumes and Cover Letters. New York: Kaplan Business, 2004.

Griffin, Jack. *How to Say It at Work: Power Words, Phrases, and Communication Secrets for Getting Ahead.* 2d ed. Upper Saddle River, N.J.: Prentice Hall Press, 2008.

Ireland, Susan. *The Complete Idiot's Guide to the Perfect Resume.* 4th ed. New York: Alpha, 2006.

Jovin, Ellen. *Email Etiquette for Business Professionals.* New York: Syntaxis Press, 2007.

Kahane, Adam. *Solving Tough Problems: An Open Way of Talking, Listening, and Creating New Realities.* 2d ed. San Francisco: Berrett-Koehler Publishers, 2007.

Karr, Ron, and Don Blohowiak. *Complete Idiot's Guide to Great Customer Service.* New York: Alpha, 2003.

Kennedy, Joyce Lain. *Cover Letters For Dummies.* Hoboken, N.J.: For Dummies, 2009.

———. *Resumes For Dummies.* 5th ed. Hoboken, N.J.: For Dummies, 2007.

Klaus, Peggy. *The Hard Truth About Soft Skills: Workplace Lessons Smart People Wish They'd Learned Sooner.* New York: Collins Business, 2008.

Miller, Patrick W. *Body Language on the Job.* Munster, Ind.: Patrick W. Miller & Associates, 2006.

Noble, David F. *Gallery of Best Cover Letters: Collection of Quality Cover Letters by Professional Resume*

Writers. 3d ed. Indianapolis, Ind.: JIST Works, 2007.

Oliu, Walter E., Charles T. Brusaw, and Gerald J. Alred. *Writing That Works: Communicating Effectively on the Job*. 9th ed. Boston: Bedford/St. Martin's, 2006.

Olsen Laney, Marti. *The Introvert Advantage: How to Thrive in an Extrovert World*. New York: Workman Publishing Company, 2002.

Reiman, Tonya. *The Power of Body Language*. New York: Pocket, 2007.

Rozakis, Laurie E. *The Complete Idiot's Guide to Grammar and Style*. 2d ed. New York: Alpha, 2003.

Shertzer, Margaret. *The Elements of Grammar*. Reading, Mass.: Longman, 1996.

Simons, Warren, and Rose Curtis. *The Resume.Com Guide to Writing Unbeatable Resumes*. New York: McGraw-Hill, 2004.

Strunk, William Jr., and E. B. White. *The Elements of Style*. 4th ed. Boston: Allyn & Beacon, 2000.

Truss, Lynne. *Eats, Shoots & Leaves: The Zero Tolerance Approach to Punctuation*. New York: Gotham Books, 2006.

University of Chicago. *The Chicago Manual of Style: The Essential Guide for Writers, Editors, and Publishers*. 15th ed. Chicago: The University of Chicago Press, 2003.

Wallace, Richard. *The Only Resume and Cover Letter Book You'll Ever Need: 600 Resumes for All Industries, 600 Cover Letters for Every Situation, 150 Positions from Entry Level to CEO.* Cincinnati, Ohio: Adams Media, 2008.

Walsh, Bill. *The Elephants of Style: A Trunkload of Tips on the Big Issues and Gray Areas of Contemporary American English.* New York: McGraw-Hill, 2004.

Yate, Martin. *Knock 'em Dead Cover Letters: Features the Latest Information on: Online Postings, Email Techniques, and Follow-up Strategies.* 8th ed. Cincinnati, Ohio: Adams Media, 2008.

Zeoli, Richard. *The 7 Principles of Public Speaking: Proven Methods from a PR Professional.* New York: Skyhorse Publishing, 2008.

Index